Together We Can

Deal with Life
in the 80's

by

ald allen

RON JENSON

with Chuck MacDonald

HERE'S LIFE PUBLISHERS, INC.

SAN BERNARDINO, CA 92402

TOGETHER WE CAN
Deal With Life in the 80's
By Ron Jenson
with Chuck MacDonald

A Campus Crusade for Christ Book
Published by
HERE'S LIFE PUBLISHERS, INC.
P.O. Box 1576
San Bernardino, CA 92402

ISBN 0-86605-001-9
Library of Congress Catalogue Card 81-86296
Product No. 40-294-1
©Copyright 1982, Campus Crusade for Christ, Inc.
All rights reserved

Printed in the United States of America.

FOR MORE INFORMATION, WRITE:

L. I. F. E. — P. O. Box A399, Sydney South 2000, Australia
Campus Crusade for Christ of Canada — Box 368, Abbottsford, B. C., V25 4N9, Canada
Campus Crusade for Christ — 103 Friar Street, Reading RGI IEP, Berkshire, England
Campus Crusade for Christ — 28 Westmoreland St., Dublin 2, Ireland
Lay Institute for Evangelism — P. O. Box 8786, Auckland 3, New Zealand
Life Ministry — P. O. Box / Bus 91015, Auckland Park 2006, Republic of So. Africa
Campus Crusade for Christ, Int'l. — Arrowhead Springs, San Bernardino, CA 92414, U.S.A.

Contents

Preface

Acknowledgments

Foreword

Introduction

DR. RONALD A. JENSON

PREFACE

Having been exercised for some time over the steady erosion of our society, I have felt a need to study this problem and make my findings and conclusions available to those who might be stirred to positive action.

Though I mention a number of negative trends in our society, I have sought to be solution-oriented. As you read the book, I encourage you to follow the "glance/gaze" approach. *Glance* at the problems; become informed, but do not concentrate there. *Gaze* at the solutions—become aware—become intelligent and articulate in your practical responses.

If you follow this counsel, I believe you will be able to become informed and inspired, and motivated to be an active part of the solutions.

Furthermore, I realize it is extremely difficult to deal with so many complex issues in survey form. These various topics deserve much fuller attention and treatment in a thoroughly researched work. However, I have tried to present a practical overview of the world scene, staying away from over-generalizations yet taking a stand on issues. May you read the book from this perspective.

ACKNOWLEDGMENTS

MY GRATEFUL THANKS AND APPRECIATION

TO THOSE WHO HAVE HELPED ME

WITH THIS BOOK

To Marc Chandler, Rayna Elmendorf and Lynette Landfear, who helped me stay on top of all my projects, providing a joyous atmosphere in which to work.

To Jim Mulkey, Senator Bill Armstrong, Arch Decker, Bob Pyke, Carl Wilson, Alan Scholes, Lane Adams and Tim Timmons for their helpful suggestions about content and style.

To Bill Bright for his constant support and encouragement.

To Dave Enlow and Jean Bryant for their masterful copy editing.

To my wife Mary for her love and devotion.

And mostly to Chuck MacDonald for his patience and invaluable assistance in taking my raw research and dictation and breathing literary life into it.

FOREWORD

In 1977, I had a chance to observe the ministry of Ron Jenson. Ron was a successful pastor in Philadelphia at the time. In addition to his duties with a rapidly growing church, Ron was the dean of the Christian Leadership Training Center, a ministry of Campus Crusade for Christ to a group of 75 pastors from 22 denominations.

In cooperation with Carl Combs, our Philadelphia director, Ron was giving direction to the group and helping to train them in management, church growth and other areas. I was greatly impressed with his leadership abilities, his warmth and his commitment to our Lord.

A year later, the ministry of Campus Crusade for Christ was ready to launch a School of Theology which, in addition to training students for Christian leadership, would provide the ethical foundation as well as the umbrella for the International Christian Graduate University.

Because of the crucial nature of this school, we prayed for a president who would be an outstanding leader with a burning heart for God. We wanted a scholar who was a powerful communicator, a churchman, an evangelist and a discipler of men. As we sought for the man with these qualifications, it soon became apparent that such a man was already involved with us in training pastors. It was obvious that Ron Jenson was the man for the job.

Ron accepted the presidency of the International School of Theology in 1978 and has given outstanding leadership to it from the beginning. One of the issues that he has endeavored to impress upon the student body is the need for the Christians of America to act as the salt of the earth and the light of the world. Ron believes, as I do, that there is a great paradox in our land where, according to the Gallup Poll, approximately one-third of the adult population claims to be "born again," yet, tragically, there seems to be very little Christian influence in our society.

In this excellent book, TOGETHER WE CAN, Ron describes the perilous times in which we live, but he does not stop there. He gives positive steps of action that we can take to help reverse the distressing trends we see everywhere around us. He shows us that together, as believers, we can make a difference in helping to turn our nation back to God. I believe you will find TOGETHER WE CAN stimulating and motivational reading. I recommend it to you highly.

Bill Bright
Arrowhead Springs

INTRODUCTION

America and the world stand at a crossroads today. This nation and other nations are experiencing problems that are unprecedented in their history. Seldom have as many countries of the world been without direction.

This global crisis is affecting millions of men, women and children. And if trends existing today are not reversed, the negative impact on people everywhere will continue to accelerate. Even in the early years of this country when we were facing attack from our opponents abroad, the danger was not as great as it is today. Then our national morale was high; today it has fallen. Then the moral fiber of America was strong; today it is not.

As Arthur Koestler put it, "Nature has let us down, God seems to have left the receiver off the hook, the time is running out." Joan Baez echoes the thought, "You are the orphans in an age of no tomorrows."

Is there any path from this crossroads that does not lead downward to despair and oblivion? Will your country—and mine—join the other great nations of history which have collapsed from within? In spite of distressing signs all around us, I believe there is a path that can take us away from despair. Our spiral toward defeat can be halted if Christians truly will become the "salt of the earth."

During the period of history when Jesus first spoke to His followers of this concept, salt served as a preserving agent for food. In today's society, as Christians live in the power of God's Spirit, their individual and corporate lifestyles will serve as preserving salt in a society plagued by corruption. Our society shows a lack of "saltiness" despite the fact that some 84 million adults label themselves as "born again."

Why? In this book, we will examine this lack of saltiness in the Church as well as the deterioration of the major institutions that have historically given direction to society. In addition, we will look at the underlying reason for the impairment of these institutions, which is a flawed philosophy of life.

It is my fervent hope that as you read this book, a turning of purpose will begin—in your own heart—and spread to those around you. It is only as this happens in the lives of Christians that once again the Church will be returned to its proper position of influence in society. You can have a part in making an impact that will affect you first, then become national and global — a redirection of life and effort. *Together we can.*

RON JENSON

Arrowhead Springs, Calif.

CHAPTER ONE

A Glance at the Problem

> Dear Ann Landers: I don't care what you do with this letter.
> You don't even have to read it if you don't want to, but I have
> to write it. A lot of people wonder why anyone would want to
> commit suicide. Most of us have a decent life and so it seems
> like a crazy thing to do. But it doesn't seem so crazy to me.
> I'm a guy who wishes he didn't have to get up every morning
> and face the day. I'm 17 years old and a junior in high school.
> I'm empty, useless and tired of struggling. I feel like I'm in
> everybody's way...I have no idea why I was born. I don't fit in
> anyplace. I know you can't do anything about all this, but I
> wanted to explain to somebody what goes through a per-
> son's mind before he pulls the trigger or swallows one too
> many pills. (Signed) A nonperson![1]

This letter to newspaper columnist Ann Landers reflects
the sense of ultimate despair present in our society today.
Many people see themselves as nonpersons. Some have no
direction; they have thrown out the past, saying history
has no meaning. Some throw out the future, or fear it,
because so much of what they see in our culture is
cultivating the negative. From a non-spiritual viewpoint,
there are few positive signs in our future.

Many observers feel we have passed the point of no
return. Norman O. Brown says, "Today even the survival
of humanity is a utopian hope." In *Building the City of
Man*, W. Warren Wagar writes of 20th-century man as "a
baby in a wicker basket, wailing on the doorstep of
doomsday." Historian Arnold Toynbee predicts an
emerging world government which, he concedes, will have
to be dictatorial. The outlook for man and the humanistic
society which he has created is bleak, but *there is a way
out.*

There is no question that the world is in trouble. But in
spite of the problems that face us, a road lies open to us that

can lead away from destruction to new life. This is the path that leads toward moral and spiritual strength. It is a path that some have trod before.

America, for example, was following in that path in the 1800's when a French historian and political theorist, Alexis de Tocqueville, visited the United States and sought to discover the greatness and genius of this country. De Tocqueville observed the great natural resources of the country including its rivers, fields, mines and vast world commerce, but did not see them to be the key to the nation's greatness.

> Not until I went into the churches of America, and heard her pulpits aflame with righteousness did I understand the secrets of her genius and power. America is great because she is good, and if America ever ceases to be good, America will cease to be great![2]

This nation has ceased to be great, and it is because it has ceased to be good. But it doesn't have to continue on that road—nor does your homeland. Our society's disintegration can be stopped if Christians will follow Christ's command to be the "salt of the earth."

If Christians do not become the salt of the earth, our world is doomed. If Christians do not help to choose the path at the crossroads that leads in the direction of moral and spiritual awakening, there is little hope for the world. General Douglas McArthur outlined the consequences of this choice:

> History fails to record a single precedent in which nations subject to moral decay have not passed into political and economic decline. There has been either a spiritual awakening to overcome the moral lapse, or a progressive deterioration leading to ultimate national disaster.[3]

Nowhere is this impending disaster more evident than in the rapid deterioration of five basic institutions that give direction to society: family, education, media, government and religion.

Family Life Disintegrating

Marriages are falling apart at a rate never before experienced. Some 38 percent of all first marriages fail today, and that number is increasing rapidly. Seventy-nine percent of those people will remarry and 44 percent of those will divorce again. Even Christian marriages are ending in divorce in unparalleled numbers.

One of the major reasons for this is that the commitment to the institution of marriage has been virtually wiped out. Men and women believe that divorce is a viable option. Many don't really mean the words, "Till death do us part," which they recite in their marriage ceremony.

Another reason marriage is in such crisis today is because Christian marriages have not demonstrated oneness. Even of those Christians who don't get divorced today, many experience emotional divorce. Many disgruntled people simply shut their spouses out of their lives and live in their own emotional worlds.

A man and a woman have a romantic experience, they make a commitment to another (more often than not emotionally), and then the husband goes one way and the wife goes another. They immediately start to live their lives as married singles. They experience no warmth, no unity, no oneness. Their relationship is only a shadow of what God intended.

Another reason for crisis in marriages today is the existence of pre-marital and extra-marital sex. God's intent has always been one man-one woman. He intended men and women to come together and be one in their marriage relationship. When a person has sexual relations with another *before* marriage, he has tremendous guilt *in* marriage. The psychological implications are staggering. I have spent many hours in marital counseling with people who are just trying to handle the guilt from their own pre-marital and extra-marital experiences. God hates pre-marital and extra-marital sex, and to be involved in it is going to hurt any marriage it touches.

As a result of the problems in marriage, family life is suffering. One-half of all the children in America today will spend the major portion of their childhood living with a single parent. Most of these children will be living with their mothers. This has a devastating effect upon the children. God intended that a child be developed by both a man and a woman. Because of the bitterness, frustration and defeat of divorce, these children are not being developed by both parents, and in turn easily can develop their own bitterness and depression along with other serious problems.

Even in those families where parents are living together, the father frequently doesn't carry out his responsibilities. It is estimated that the average father spends only 37 seconds a day with each child.[4] This is in direct contrast to the scriptural command to bring up the children in the nurture and admonition of the Lord. That simply cannot be accomplished in 37 seconds a day!

Another concept that is destructive to the family is the well-hidden purpose behind such things as the Year of the Child. The government is aware of the high rate of child abuse and single parent homes. So the government has become increasingly involved in the area of the family.

The sense of responsibility felt by the husband and the wife decreases because their children can be taken care of by government-paid child care institutions. As a result, that responsibility is shifted significantly to the government. The family loses its effect bit by bit, even though the parents may feel they are honestly attempting to deal with the problems. Governmental intrusion into the family will not be stopped until a dramatic moral change in the lives of our families takes place.

Education

Another major institution in America that is deteriorating is education. Dr. Charles Malik, an educator who holds more than 50 degrees and was one of the founders of the United Nations, says that the major problem in this nation today is the philosophy of atheistic humanism being taught in our universities.

> Nothing compares with the urgency of seeking to recapture the universities for Jesus Christ. The universities have divorced the excellence of the mind from the excellence of spirit and character. Christ is not welcome in the university. In fact, He is ignored, if not declared the enemy. This estrangement, if not downright enmity, between Christ and the great universities, cannot continue without disastrous results upon the whole of western civilization. [5]

The atheistic humanism that is being taught so diligently at our universities as well as in our other schools teaches that man is the center of the universe. This religion holds that man does not really need God, since he has within himself and his technology all that he needs to make himself and his life meaningful.

Since man is basically good, say many secular humanists, society will evolve to a better and better existence. This anti-biblical teaching is being impressed on the minds of students at all levels of education today. As a result, education is on a downhill trend like never before, as we shall see in a later chapter.

This downward trend is reflected in the emergence of three devastating forces in our education system. One of these forces is the unparalleled violence in the classrooms of America.

In 1972 the *American School Board Journal* reported that teaching school is twice as dangerous as working in a steel mill. It's estimated that each year 75,000 teachers are injured badly enough to require medical attention.

According to the Senate Sub-committee on Juvenile Delinquency, between 1964 and 1968, assaults on teachers increased 7,100% and are increasing at even greater rates today. [6]

The second devastating trend in our education system is its diminishing sense of values. Most people who have graduated from high school or college in the last few years have grown up in an educational system that was not based upon ethical values at all. When this country began, more than 98 percent of the education was based on very clear moral absolutes. But today, *absolute* is a bad word. Everything is relative.

If I say there are absolutes, I am accused of being narrow. Because everything is seen as relative, we do not communicate in absolute values. More often than not, students are being influenced by the values of their teachers which tend to be based on humanism rather than biblical truths. This develops an attitude within the students that leads them to an unbiblical world view.

Another problem is that the classroom is no longer the key teaching agent in our society—the media is. An estimated 330 new magazines were begun in America in 1976. Most of them were geared to the teen generation and filled with a permissive, humanistic world view.

Media

This trend of deterioration is pronounced in the third
major institution — the media. Television in particular has
dulled the senses of people. The A.C. Nielsen Co. reveals
that the average household had its television set on for 6
hours and 36 minutes each day during 1980. A result of this
continued exposure to television is that we are finding all
sorts of subtle desires developed within us of which we're
not even aware.

According to the Annenberg School of Communication's George Gerbner, television portrays an average of 5.6
violent acts per hour, which skyrockets to 18 per hour
during the slam-bang action on children's shows. Before
the age of 15, an average child will have witnessed between
11,000, and 13,000 acts of violence including assaults,
rapes, murders, robberies and other assorted mayhem in
every conceivable variety using every kind of weapon. This
continued exposure to violence can have disastrous effects.

Consider James R. Groenveld, a 16-year-old, who re-
enacted a Russian roulette scene he had viewed in the
movie "The Deer Hunter." The result of his action was that
he died from a gunshot wound to his right temple.

Another instance of media violence inspiring real-life
violence is the story of a 4-year-old girl named Khonji
Wilson who was killed by her own mother after the two
watched Exorcist II on television. Mrs. Wilson, believing
Khonji to be demon-possessed, stabbed her daughter to
death and then cut her heart out. The movie had contained
a similar scene, where a small girl's heart was cut out to rid
her of a demon.

Government

The fourth major institution that is deteriorating in this
nation today is the government. In recent years one of the
major problems in our government has been a burgeoning
bureaucracy. This expensive package of bureaucracy in the
United States comes lavishly wrapped in red tape. It costs
business and industry and ultimately the consumer almost
$20 billion a year to handle the paperwork involved with
government regulations. It costs government and thus the

consumer another $20 billion a year to pay for its printers, processors and paper shufflers.

That's $40 billion a year for triplicate forms, filing cabinets, postage stamps and waste paper baskets! Most of it is counter-productive. *U.S. News & World Report* observed that wrathful constituents were bombarding congressmen with protests against such federally funded projects as $375,000 for a Pentagon study of the frisbee, $80,000 to develop a zero-gravity toilet, $121,000 to find out why some people say "ain't" and $29,000 for a study on the mating calls of the Central American toad. These are just a few examples of how the taxpayers' money has been wasted.

Other examples of waste and inefficiency in government include $600,000 in subsidy payments given to a single beekeeper in Washington, D.C.; millions of dollars paid out annually to ineligible welfare recipients; and $85,000 per minute wasted to pay interest on the national debt.[7]

Unquestionably government is in a mess. You can hardly pick up a newspaper without reading about wrongdoing in government. As a result of this corruption, most people don't respect government officials. Because of this loss of faith in government, people don't vote and don't want to get involved because they don't think there is any solution to the problem.

As a result of the bureaucracy and the inability of the people to trust government leaders, there is a corresponding inability for government to move decisively in foreign situations. Many feel this has resulted in the Soviet Union gaining military superiority. This fact is acknowledged by no less an authority than Dr. Henry Kissinger in an article in the September 2, 1979 issue of the *Detroit News:*

> If present trends continue, the 1980's will be a period of massive crisis for all of us, Kissinger told a symposium on the future of NATO. The dominant fact of the current military situation is that the NATO countries are falling behind in every significant category. Never in history has it happened that a nation achieved superiority in all significant weapons categories without seeking to translate this at some point into some foreign-policy benefit.

Obviously, Dr. Kissinger and others expect the Russians to use this military might they've amassed to further their plans of world Communism.

As a result of our indecision in foreign affairs and our lack of a cogent, long-term foreign policy, we have allowed the Soviet Union to move close to our nuclear capabilities and perhaps exceed them in certain areas.

Religion

The family, education, media and government are falling apart. And finally, religion too is disintegrating.

Significant interest in religion pervades the nation today, but much of it is not in biblical Christianity. People are interested in spiritual experience, which can take the form of humanistic, man-made religion on the one hand, or mysticism — like Hare Krishna — on the other hand. Both of these extremes are attempts to deal with the problems some people see as rampant in our society.

In addition to these points of view, there are two more extremes within Christianity. One is liberalism. Many of the churches today, particularly mainline denominations, fall into this category. There is no single denomination that holds this position completely, but many tend toward a liberal or neo-orthodox position. People holding these positions do not believe in the biblical emphasis on the deity of Christ or the Bible as the infallible Word of God.

On the other extreme is what I call pietistic, experiential evangelicalism. These are some of the people who are becoming "born-again." Gallup says more than 84 million Americans claim to have had a religious experience and most label it a "born again" experience. Many people are coming to Christ today, but a significant number are not absorbing the principles of Scripture. Consequently, they are not becoming the "salt of the earth."

One of the major ways we evangelical Christians have manifested this pseudo-pietism is through our lack of intense and meaningful involvement in solving the social ills of our day. We've left this activity to more liberally-minded churchmen. What a tragedy! It is as though such involvement would be unspiritual. Think of it...caring for the real needs of people as being unspiritual.

Scripture punctures this myth *beautifully* and powerfully:

"Pure religion is this, to visit the widows and homeless..." (James 5 NAS).

"He who is kind to the poor lends to the Lord" (Proverbs. 19:17).

"I know that the Lord maintains the cause of the afflicted, and executed justice for the needy" (Psalm 140:12).

"And you shall answer and say before the Lord your God, My Father was a wandering Aramean and he went down to Egypt and sojourned there, few in number; but there he became a great, mighty and populous nations. And the Egyptians treated us harshly and afflicted us, and imposed hard labor on us. Then we cried to the Lord, the God of our fathers and the Lord heard our voice and saw our affliction and our toil and our oppression; and the Lord brought us out of Egypt with a mighty hand and an outstretched arm and with great terror and with signs and wonders" (Deuteronomy 26:5-8).

"Woe to those who enact evil statutes, And to those who constantly record unjust decisions, so as to deprive the needy of justice and rob the poor of My people of their rights in order that widows may be their spoil, and that they may plunder the orphans. Now what will you do in the day of punishment, and in the devastation which will come from afar? To whom will you flee for help? And where will you leave your wealth? Nothing remains but to crouch among the captives or fall among the slain. In spite of all this His anger does not turn away, And his hand is still stretched out" (Isaiah 10:1-4).

"For wicked men are found among My people, They watch like fowlers lying in wait; They set a trap, they catch men. Like a cage full of birds, so their houses are full of deceit; therefore they have become great and rich. They are fat, they are sleek, they also excel in deeds of wickedness; they do not plead the cause, the cause of the orphan, that they may prosper; and they do not defend the rights of the poor. Shall I not punish these people? declares the Lord, on a nation such as this shall I not avenge Myself?" (Jeremiah 5:26-29).

"For if you truly amend your ways and your deeds, if you truly practice justice between a man and his neighbor, if you do not oppress the alien, the orphan, or the widow, and do not shed innocent blood in this place nor walk after other gods to your own ruin, then I will let you dwell in this place in the land that I gave to your fathers forever and ever" (Jeremiah 7:5-7).

"The Spirit of the Lord is upon Me because He anointed Me to preach the gospel to the poor. He has sent me to proclaim release to the captives and recovery of sight to the blind, To set free those

who are downtrodden to proclaim the favorable year of the Lord"
(Luke 4: 18, 19).

"Thou has seen it, for Thou hast beheld mischief and vexation to
take it into Thy hand. The unfortunate commits himself to Thee;
Thou hast been the helper of the orphan....O Lord, Thou hast
heard the desire of the humble; Thou wilt incline Thine ear to
vindicate the orphan and the oppressed, that man who is of the
earth may cause terror no more" (Psalm 10:14,17,18).

"And He also went on to say to the one who had invited Him,
'When you give a luncheon or a dinner, do not invite your friends
or your brothers or your relatives or rich neighbors, lest they also
invite you in return, and repayment come to you. But when you
give a reception, invite the poor, the crippled, the lame, the blind,
and you will be blessed, since they do not have the means to repay
you; for you will be repaid at the resurrection of the righteous"
(Luke 14:12-14).

"Wash yourselves, make yourselves clean; Remove the evil of your
deeds from My sight. Cease to do evil, Learn to do good; seek
justice, Reprove the ruthless; defend the orphan, plead for the
widow" (Isaiah 1:16,17).

"For the Lord your God is the God of gods and the Lord of lords, the
great, the mighty and the awesome God who does not show
partiality nor take a bribe. He executes justice for the orphan and
the widow and shows His love for the alien by giving him food and
clothing" (Deuteronomy 10:17,18).

"For the poor will never cease to be in the land; therefore I command you, saying, 'You shall freely open your hand to your
brother, to your needy and poor in your land' " (Deuteronomy
15:11).

God's commitment to the needy is seen in His overt and
vivid identification with them.

"He who oppresses the poor reproaches his Maker, But he who is
gracious to the needy honors Him" (Proverbs 14:31).

"He who is gracious to a poor man lends to the Lord, And He will
repay him for his good deed" (Proverbs 19:17).

"For I was hungry and you gave Me something to eat; I was thirsty,
and you gave Me drink; I was a stranger and you invited Me in;
naked, and you clothed Me; I was sick, and you came to Me; I was
in prison, and you came to Me. Then the righteous will answer
Him, saying, 'Lord, when did we see You hungry, and feed You, or
thirsty, and give You drink? and when did we see You a stranger,
and invite You in, or naked, and clothe You? And when did we see
You sick, or in prison, and come to You?' And the King will answer
and say to them, 'Truly I say to you, to the extent that you did it to

one of these brothers of Mine, even the least of them, you did it to Me" (Matthew 25:35-40).

"For you know the grace of our Lord Jesus Christ, that though He was rich, yet for your sake He became poor, that you through His poverty might become rich" (II Corinthians 8:9).

John F. Alexander states that "the fatherless, widows, and foreigners each have about forty verses that command justice for them. God wants to make it very clear that in a special sense He is the protector of these weak ones. Strangers are to be treated nearly the same as Jews, and woe to people who take advantage of orphans or widows" ("The Bible and the Other Side," *The Other Side*, 11, No. 5, Sept-Oct. 1975, p.57).

Ronald J. Sider in his penetrating book, *Rich Christians in an Age of Hunger*, states, "Regardless of what we do or say at 11:00 a.m. Sunday morning, affluent people who neglect the poor are not the people of God" (IVP—Downers Grove, Ill. 1977, p.82). Though I do not agree with all the author says, he gives a strong and convincing argument on the place of social concern, especially poverty, in our lives. This may seem like an overstatement to you but no one can deny that there is a clear, scriptural emphasis on the need for every Christian to be involved in helping to alleviate social concern. If we did as Scripture commands, we would see our society deeply impacted. Sen. Mark Hatfield has stated, "If every church in America took responsibility for two people in poverty and eight widows, these problems would be solved."

I thank God for such evangelical ministries and people as the Voice of Calvary (John Perkins), E.V. Hill, and S.T.E.P. efforts on a local and national level. They are making a substantial contribution toward solving social ills. But, we must all get involved and get involved now. No longer can we be uninvolved because we are immersed in a pseudo-pietism. Television can be guilty of feeding this pseudo-pietism.

Although I praise God for Christian television shows, too many new believers are depending upon this medium for their total source of Christian training instead of the Word of God. Because of this they are not living total

Christian lives, and as a result they are having a minimal influence in their society.

God wants us to be discerning about our activities. He doesn't want us to look at an objectionable television show and simply ignore it. He doesn't want us to go to questionable movies just because there is a cultural push or peer pressure to go. He doesn't want us to read certain pieces of literature just because other people are doing it.

He doesn't want us to respond to political and social issues the same way the rest of the world does. He wants us think biblically. He wants us to grow in real knowledge and discernment, in order that we might be able to discern what is of God and His kingdom and what is of Satan and the world, insofar as it is possible to distinguish them from the grey areas.

We need to see revival and reawakening in the Church. Then we will see change in the major institutions of our society that are collapsing around us. At one time, England was in a condition similar to that of our nation today. Then revival broke out through John Wesley's ministry. He stimulated an attack on the decay in government, business and the church.

Even though only a small percentage of the population was converted during Wesley's 50-year ministry, the face of England was changed as the handful became the salt of the earth. That small group of people not only received Christ, but were radically transformed by the reality of His Lordship in their lives. They lived a Christian lifestyle and dealt with issues in their society.

As that handful became the salt of the earth, the slave trade was stopped, four our of five taverns in certain areas were closed for lack of business, prison and penal reforms were instituted, child labor laws were improved and corruption in government declined. The key to all of this was a deep-rooted moral and spiritual awakening which had taken place.

That's what has to happen today. We not only need to see people come to Jesus Christ, but we also need to see men and women *transformed* by the power of Jesus Christ We need to be living holy, godly lives like never before and articulating the biblical response to issues in our society today.

Action Points

Begin searching the Word of God and key Christian books on the importance of being the salt of the earth in the major institutions of our society.

CHAPTER TWO

The Humanistic World View

More than any other time in history, mankind faces a cross-roads. One path leads to despair and utter hopelessness, the other to total extinction. Let us pray we have the wisdom to choose correctly. I speak, by the way, not with any sense of futility, but with a panicky conviction of the absolute mean-inglessness of existence, which could easily be misin-terpreted as pessimism. It is not. It is merely a healthy concern for the predicament of modern man.[1]

We think of Woody Allen as the master comic, but his comment reveals a serious look at today's troubled society. I too am concerned about the predicament of modern man. I too see paths leading to despair and extinction. But I also see a path leading to hope, renewal and vitality for our nation. It is a path that leads through the archway of commitment—commitment to God's purposes in every aspect of life.

In the last chapter we looked briefly at the deterioration of the major institutions in our nation. I also mentioned how humanistic influences have spread in these in-stitutions and have contributed to the difficulties we have been experiencing as a nation.

The potential collapse of these institutions is foreboding, but not as catastrophic as the world view held by the general public. "What is world view?" you ask.

Your world view, of course, is how you view the world. It is the set of presuppositions—that which is believed beforehand—which underlies all of our decisions and actions. These presuppositions (our world view) determine our thinking patterns, which in turn influence our actions.

Many factors contribute to our world view including peer pressure, parents, education, mass media, the Bible, church and other forces. Our world view may be conscious or unconscious, but it determines our destiny and the destiny of the society we live in.

Unfortunately, too many people view our world today through the glasses of humanism. As Dr. Francis Schaeffer and Dr. C. Everett Koop state, "In our time, humanism has replaced Christianity as the consensus of the West."[2]

This flawed world view is the source of the difficulties in which this nation finds itself. The decline of our major institutions is only symptomatic of the problem.

Today's battles are being waged in the mind and in the spirit, long before the results of these battles become evident in such tangible issues as economic problems, family break-ups, educational decline and others. The mind is the battleground.

The Bible points out the importance of gaining victory in this area. Proverbs 23:7 states: "For as he thinks within himself, so he is." This verse points out that how a person thinks will influence the kind of individual he will become. This theme also is the basis for a well-known adage:

Sow a thought; reap an action.
Sow an action; reap a habit.
Sow a habit; reap a character.
Sow a character; reap a destiny.

Our most important battles are being won or lost in our minds, where our world views are formed, but many people and most leaders do not recognize this. Instead they focus on the symptoms of the problem, while the real problem — the erroneous world view — continues to prevail, creating new and more complex symptoms.

The world view of the American people has resulted in numerous crises. During his term in office as President, Jimmy Carter reflected on the cause of some of these crises: "All the legislation in the world cannot fix what is wrong with America. It is a crisis of confidence, it's a crisis that strikes at the very heart, soul and spirit of our national world, and it is threatening to destroy the social and political fabric of America."

This world view of secular humanism which our nation has adopted bears examining. It discounts the supernatural and makes man the measure of all things. As we look closely at the dangerous philosophy of secular humanism, let us begin by trying to avoid confusing it with "humane," "humanitarian" and "the humanities."

"Humane" is that which is marked by compassion, sympathy or consideration for other human beings or animals. A "humanitarian" is a person promoting human welfare and social reform. "The humanities" are the branches of learning having primarily a cultural character.[3]

Humanism in a technical sense is defined and explained in the *Humanist Manifesto II* which was written in 1973 and endorsed by thousands of humanists both in this nation and abroad. To them, humanism is a philosophy of life that will "tap the creativity of each human being and provide the vision and courage for us to work together."[4] They believe humanism "can provide the purpose and inspiration that so many seek; it can give personal meaning and significance to human life."[5]

Although their objectives may be worthwhile goals, humanists leave God the Father and the Lord Jesus Christ completely out of their philosophy. They are concerned only with humans.

The secular humanists who drafted the *Humanist Manifesto* completely deny the existence of God. "We find insufficient evidence for belief in the existence of a supernatural; it is either meaningless or irrelevant to the question of survival and fulfillment of the human race. As non-theists, we begin with humans, not God—nature, not deity."

The document goes on to state, "Promises of immortal salvation or fear of eternal damnation are both illusory and harmful. They distract humans from present concerns, from self-actualization, and from rectifying social injustices."

Other foundational doctrines of humanism include organic evolution, the establishment of a one-world government, the right to express individual sexual preferences as desired, the right to suicide, abortion and euthanasia. Most true humanists also do not believe in any absolute standards of morality, relying on the situation to dictate the morality of an action.

These humanistic ideals have become deeply entrenched in our society. For instance, humanism is non-theistic (their label) which means they deny the existence of God.

In today's society, an atheist is the embodiment of this tenet. The Society of Separationists, the most visible group promoting atheism as its major doctrine, was founded by Madalyn Murray O'Hair in 1963. It boasts a membership of 60,000. It was O'Hair who was instrumental in the court decision which many people have misinterpreted as prohibiting prayer in public schools. The group's current goals include the eradication of "In God We Trust" as our national motto.[6]

A close cousin to atheism is secularism, which rejects any form of religious faith and worship. Materialism is another close relative. This philosophy holds that only matter exists; there is no supernatural. The practical outworking of these two philosophies is that people believing in them concern themselves totally with secular pursuits, becoming preoccupied with acquiring material possessions.

Evidence for materialism is on all sides of us in this consumer-conscious, "keep-up-with-the Joneses" society. An article in the May 28, 1979 issue of *Time* took a look at the segment of the population born immediately after World War II.

> These baby boomers are "the children of inflation, born with credit cards in their mouths and oriented toward spending rather than saving. They are part of the instant-gratification, self-indulgent Me generation, which has a taste for high-priced gadgets and little interest in self-denial."

Experts estimate that this 35-to-44 age group spends 50% more than the average consumer for furniture, one-third more for appliances and buys 25% of all vans and pickups. Says Louis W. Stern, marketing professor at Northwestern University: "That age group wants the outward visible things that say, 'I have made it and I want to live comfortably.'"

Another humanist tenet is the belief that there are

no absolute standards. This article of faith is embraced by a wide variety of people, but is especially prevalent in educational circles. At one meeting of 400 college and university presidents, most agreed that nothing is absolutely right or nothing is absolutely wrong. They did agree, however on one absolute: belief in absolute academic freedom. In other words, they'll believe in absolutes when they serve their purposes.[7]

Humanism has been spreading its tentacles throughout our nation for many years and has begun to strangle many of our institutions, especially the field of education. But it has only been recently that the general public has been made aware of humanism, and its subtle, yet powerful influence on the thinking of this nation.

Noted Russian author Alexandr Solzhenitsyn forcefully brought humanism into the public eye through a commencement address he gave to the 1978 graduating class of Harvard University. Solzhenitsyn criticized Western values and proclaimed that "destructive and irresponsible individual freedom has been granted boundless space."

The primary problem, in Solzhenitsyn's opinion, was the rise of humanism: "Such a tilt of freedom in the direction of evil has come about gradually, but it was evidently born out of a humanistic and benevolent concept according to which there is no evil inherent to human nature; the world belongs to mankind and all the defects of life are caused by wrong social systems which must be corrected."

Solzhenitsyn's comments created a stir in the media while echoing a conviction held by an increasing number of evangelical Christians: that, even though most Americans express a belief in God, our society has lost its Judeo-Christian base.

The primary influence of humanism has been to cause people to take their eyes off God and to rely on human resources to solve problems. Many people believe in God, but are practicing humanists. Their belief in God does not significantly influence their world view or any of the solutions they see for the world's problems.

Humanistic ideals are widely disseminated through

public education, the media and through organizations like the American Civil Liberties Union (ACLU), Sex Information and Education Council of the United States (SIECUS) and the National Organization of Women (NOW). Humanistic philosophy has become so widespread that it has subtly influenced the thinking of Christians, causing us to concentrate on our own pleasures, desires and abilities rather than on God. Hardly a person, even in the Christian community, is not affected.

The German comedian Karl Vallentin was famous for a skit which clearly illustrates the folly of the contemporary humanistic philosophies in providing man with the answers he so desperately seeks. Coming onto the stage in almost total darkness, Vallentin paced around a solitary lamp which provided a circle of light. A policeman crossed the stage, noticed Vallentin's worried look, and asked what he had lost. Vallentin answered that he had lost the key to his house. The policeman joined in the hunt.

After a while the search appeared fruitless. "Are you sure you lost it here?" asked the policeman. "Oh no!" said Vallentin. Pointing to the dark corner, he said, "I lost it over there." "Then why on earth are you looking over here?" asked the policeman. "Because there's no light over there!" replied Vallentin.

Like Vallentin, modern man is looking for answers to his problems. But his humanistic philosophies have not aided him in his search. If only he would allow the light of Christ to flood his life, man in today's society would find the solutions to his problems lying within reach.

Humanism's blanket of darkness also has shrouded the minds of many Christians today, causing them to lose a biblical perspective on a number of issues. Dan Maust, a Campus Crusade for Christ staff member since 1966, has some excellent insight into how humanism has affected the thinking of Christians. Dan presented these ideas in the March, 1981 issue of *Worldwide Challenge*.

First, he noted, humanism works to weaken the Christian's conviction of the sinfulness of man. The sinfulness of man is a central theme in the Bible. Yet many Christians today have been influenced by our humanistic world to see man as really "good," with just a few flaws.

Second, humanism produces a false hope in what man can do to bring about a world of peace and plenty. Christians must work unceasingly for a better world—a peaceful one in which poverty and hunger are eliminated. But we can be under no illusion that men alone will bring this about merely by better programs, more laws, new policies or more advanced technology. We must trust the King of the universe to motivate and empower us to bring about this transformation.

Third, humanism works to weaken moral convictions. Humanism creates a "live and let live" climate that pushes tolerance to an extreme. Consequently, as Christians we lose our sense of moral outrage at the immorality and injustice in our world.

Clearly, humanism is an insidious tenet. As the salt of the earth, we Christians must purge our lives from humanism's influences and aggresively take the offensive in eliminating it from our society.

The battle against secular humanism is not a hopeless one. For all the widespread influence of humanistic world view, the actual number of those trying to spread this philosophy in a calculated way is relatively small. According to the August 26, 1973 issue of *The New York Times*, there were only 250,000 self-described humanists in America. Allowing for a 10 percent increase, they would number about 275,000 today.[8]

But many of these individuals occupy key positions of leadership in this country and are able to use their positions to further the cause of humanism throughout the nation.

The tide can be turned, however. Contrasted with this relatively small number of self-proclaimed humanists and their resources of position and influence is the vast army of Christians with the limitless resources of a bountiful God. If this vast army can be mobilized and empowered by the Lord to be the salt of the earth and the light of the world, the battle can be won. Through a vividly godly lifestyle, through the power of the Word, through the power of the ballot, through concerned action and through unfaltering faith in a powerful God, Christians can be victorious.

Action Points

1. Become more familiar with the biblical world view. Begin to examine the Scriptures for application to your lifestyle.
2. Consider ways that our nation's humanistic world view has shaped some of your thoughts and ideas.
3. Help your children, especially teenagers, understand the various world views that will challenge their faith. Teach them to identify humanistic ideas and values. Explain why humanistic ideas are inadequate.

CHAPTER THREE

Solution Steps for the Individual

So if we do not make a change in this country soon I believe with the pressures that we face—of inflation, of redistribution of wealth in the world, of the outward pressures of Islam and Communism—I feel that the people of this country are ripe for accepting some sort of an elite—such as Daniel Bell of Harvard would suggest—just to keep the illusion of personal peace and affluence. And if Christians are going down the same road, then some of us better get down on our knees and say to God, "God, help us."—Francis Schaeffer[1]

As we have seen in previous chapters, this nation is facing some crippling problems. Our major institutions—the family, education, government, media and the church—are crumbling. And the people's humanistic world view is leading us away from solutions and into deeper difficulties.

With such complex problems, it would seem that we are without hope. But that's not true. We have cause for optimism, for enthusiasm, for excitement! Because we Christians have the inexhaustible resources of an omnipotent God at our disposal. Energized by the power of God's Spirit, Christians can advance boldly into their world serving as the salt of the earth and the light of the world in obedience to Christ's command.

As this takes place, I believe we will see dramatic changes in our institutions, in the world view of the people and in the general health of our nation. It is my desire to bring you face to face with problems in our society, then propose solution steps—specific actions that you can take to help cause renewal. "Salt of the earth" should not be a nebulous phrase, but a goal, a watchword, complete with realistic, practical steps to help make that goal a reality.

The fulfillment of this goal in the lives of Christians across this land will have a great deal to do with saving this nation from collapse. I want to see us survive because of our great history of democratic tradition and freedom.

But beyond patriotism, I want to see our nation survive because, from the point of view of resources for the Christian mission, we are a major center of the world.

The United States, including its northern neighbor, currently has some 30,300 missionaries serving other peoples or nations other than their own. This represents more than half of all the world's Christian missionaries. This nation also has a significant history of supporting and fostering missions overseas.[2]

We have great freedom to share our faith, develop strategies for reaching people for Christ and disciple them. Frequently these strategies are tested here and then adapted overseas with great success.

However, there is a lack of moral and spiritual health which begins at the individual level and radiates outward. If the individual is not healthy, it will affect the family. If the family is not healthy, it will result in an unhealthy church. And if the church is not healthy, it will affect the society. That is our situation today.

This chain reaction of change has as its detonation point the individual. Perhaps you think it is impossible for you to influence society. But, as we consider the lessons of history, some of the significant turning points in history have been engineered by a single person.

John Dewey, for instance, changed the face of education. He left the imprint of his humanistic values in our schools. And the educational system of today still feels the impact of his life.

In 1900, Nikolai Lenin organized a ragtag band of people under his political philosophy. Seventeen years later, this band of extremists gained control of the Soviet Union, the largest land mass of any nation in the world. And today millions of people groan under his political philosophy of Communism.

In 1859, Charles Darwin published *Origin of Species*. His research and findings gave rise to the theory of organic evolution which still ripples throughout the scientific and educational community today.

Great *good* can also be accomplished by a single individual. Consider the example of Martin Luther who nailed his 95 theses to the door of the Catholic church in Wittenberg. His commitment to the doctrine of "salvation by faith" resulted in a reawakening of people's interest in a personal faith. Millions of people worship today in churches that were born out of Luther's commitment.

Another example of the impact a single life can have is that of William Carey. Called "the father of Protestant missions," his example and ministry in India brought into focus the concept that Christians do have the responsibility to reach out with the gospel to those who have never heard. Generations of people in countless nations were reached by missionaries who were inspired by Carey's example.

Yes, one person can make a difference. And that is true in today's society even as it was true during the lives of these men. You can make an impact on your country!

In order to see your country held together, you need to see positive changes take place in the family, education, government and religion. But the key to influencing these societal ills is the church. It must be healthy. Similarly, for the family to be healthy, the individual needs to be healthy.

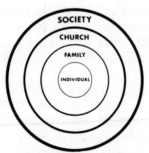

In order for one man or one woman to make a difference in our society, that person needs to consider seriously what his purpose is here on earth. In Mark 12:30, 31, Christ gave us a command relating to our purpose in life. He said, "You shall love the Lord your God with all your heart, and with all your soul, and with all your mind and with all your strength. And you shall love your neighbor as yourself."

These verses point out that our first priority is to have a

radical love relationship with God. This encompasses our total being. First, we are to love God with all of our mind. This is where the real battle takes place. It is of prime importance that I learn how to bring my mind into a love relationship with God. I do that as I saturate my mind with God's Word and as I learn to think biblically.

Christians struggle with thoughts and attitudes. Satan will constantly try to change the directions of our minds. He will stimulate impure thoughts and wrong attitudes. He will work on making us bitter—on anything he can to get our minds off track spiritually. If he can do that, he can immobilize us. And if he can do that, he can keep us from telling people about God and His kingdom.

Romans 12:2 tells us, "Do not be conformed to this world but be transformed (metamorphosis) by the renewing of your mind." The key to becoming what God wants you to become is to get the right thoughts into your mind and internalize them.

The key to getting the right things into your mind and into your life is through a biblical concept of meditation. The end product of meditation is success and that is what God wants for our lives. This is spelled out in Joshua 1:8, which says: "This book of the law shall not depart from your mouth, but you shall *meditate* on it day and night, so that you may be careful to do according to all that is written in it; for then you will make your way prosperous, and then you will have good success." This same concept is found in Psalms 1.

Now let us look at the practical working definition of the concept. Three words help define and give one an understanding of biblical meditation. The first word is *chewing.* When I meditate on Scripture I chew on it. The word meditation reflects the idea of a cow *chewing* on grass. It goes down to one compartment of the stomach to be regurgitated later. She chews on it again and it goes into another compartment of her stomach. She keeps chewing on that grass, allowing it to go into other compartments of her stomach, finally to be assimilated into the rest of her body.

This is similar to the concept of meditation. Memorize a passage of Scripture and chew on it over and over again.

Apply it to one part of your life, then bring it up, chew on it over and over again and keep applying it to other parts of your life.

The second word that applies to meditation is *analyzing.* If I am going to meditate I need to analyze the passage of Scripture, emphasize key words, look up those key words and see what they mean.

The third word relating to meditation is *action.* I need to act on what the Word of God says, to be obedient to what God's Word says, and then share it with others. God wants to use you to minister to others as the Word of God is transforming you.

One of the keys to meditation is that you need to practice it regularly. Perhaps you have an area in your life right now that is a struggle. Find a passage of Scripture related to that area and start meditating on the passage regularly — three or four times a day. When you get up, at lunch time and then again before you go to bed, try to find time to meditate.

I am sold on meditation; it is what the Word of God teaches and I have seen this principle change my life.

As a young boy, I was constantly getting into trouble. I had a poor self-concept and did not like the way I looked. People called me "Jelly-Belly Jenson." I was so rebellious that I internalized my dissatisfaction and became a frustrated, anxious, angry little boy. As a result, I got into fights all the time.

I was in trouble with the law for stealing and for forgery when I was ten years old. I was in trouble with my family. I was in trouble at school. Every place you could get in trouble, I did. It was all a manifestation of the problems within me — a poor self-concept and a poor relationship with God.

Part of my experience during that time was a struggle with lustful thoughts. So, while I was growing up as a Christian, even as I entered high school, and on into college, I struggled with my thought life. With so much junk in my mind I struggled and had trouble purifying my thought life.

To battle my besetting sin, I tried to discipline myself; I tried fasting; I tried abstinence. I tried everything I could to deal with the problems of my thought life.

It became even more acute as I rose to positions of spiritual leadership and knew that ourwardly I had everything in order, but internally I was not having victory in a major area of my life. I kept giving in, over and over again. It was a pattern I could not break.

You may not have a problem with your thought life. You may have trouble with your attitudes about money, or with relationships. You may have problems with bitterness or worry or lust for things. It could be anything. The point is that I had a besetting sin over which I could not get victory.

Then I learned about biblical meditation. I took Colossians 3:1-17 and memorized it, forwards and backwards. I meditated on it for a year, four or five times a day, every day, 10 to 15 minutes at a time. God finally worked in me so my desires to be holy and think His thoughts were greater than those to be impure and want my own way.

What happened was that I was literally "transformed by the renewing of my mind." That is what God can do. Some of you are saying, "I have sins in my life I cannot control." I am saying you *can* control them.[3]

I promise you, if you begin to meditate on the Word of God regularly, you can have consistent victory in every area of your life. But it will take a lot of hard work, and you will have to apply some other principles we will discuss later in this book. You will need to trust the power of God to work through you by faith, lest these principles become simply a legalistic code for you. You can be victorious, and no besetting sin need hold you back from an ongoing impact for eternity.

I need to love God with all my heart, soul and mind. One of the great problems today is that some people are doctrinally correct, but somehow have become mechanical—calloused to the things of God.

How can you really love the Lord? How can you begin to feel deeply about those things which God feels deeply about? You need to practice the presence of God. This involves a sense of worshiping the Lord no matter what we are doing. Whether I am in church or mowing my lawn, I need to enjoy the *PRESENCE* of God.

An acrostic of the word will give you some insight on how to practice the presence of God.

P—*Praise God continually.* This means we praise God as a way of life for who He is and what He has done. Scripture says in Psalm 22:3, "The presence of God inhabits the praise of His people."

When people corporately and individually praise God with an attitude of expectation, God is *actively* present in that expression of praise. An example is found in 2 Chronicles 20. Jehoshaphat was facing a humanly impossible situation. His nation was hopelessly outnumbered by the Moabites, the Ammonites and the inhabitants of Mount Seir. God's command was to praise Him.

As the Israelites obeyed and praised God, He worked a miracle. The invading armies began to fight among themselves and Judah was victorious without striking a single blow. It was as if when the people praised God, Satan became confused. God graciously became actively present in the situation in response to their faith expressed through praise.

Like the inhabitants of Judah, we will face impossible difficulties and problems in our lives. And when we do, we should praise God. When we praise God in difficult situations, He is free to move mightily.

R—*Rejoice in negative circumstances.* The Phillips paraphrase records James 1:2-4 this way, "When all kinds of trials and temptations crowd into your lives, my brothers, don't resent them as intruders, but welcome them as friends!" Isn't that perverse logic? He says, when you have a cold, or you can't pay your bills, or your car falls apart, you are to welcome these problems as friends. Can you imagine opening the door, spreading your arms out wide and saying, "Hi, cold, come on it, it's great to have you here!"

James goes on to explain why we are to react to problems this way. "Knowing that the testing of your faith produces patience. And let patience have its perfect result, that you may be perfect and complete, lacking in nothing" (verses 3,4).

Here is a simple equation that may help you remember this concept:

Problems + Rejoicing = Patience

Patience + Time and Repetition = Completeness

E — *Experience the Lord in your low points.* Several years ago, I attended an organizational meeting for a ministry with which I was involved. During this meeting, some of my good friends raked me over the coals. Usually I have a pretty good self-concept and can handle criticism. But this particular night I felt betrayed by my friends. I had never been so emotionally low in my life.

After driving home, I sat in front of my house in the car. It was 2 a.m. and I was emotionally, physically and spiritually drained. I could not pray and I did not want to read the Bible. Normally, when we are down, the last thing we want to do is turn to the Lord. And yet, that is the point that God wants to use in our lives to teach us great truths.

David experienced some great truths in his life because he was open before God when he was down. That was the case with me as I sat in my car. At that point, I began to cry uncontrollably. Anger, bitterness and frustration overcame me because of the events of the night. That is when God allowed me to sing the only song I could recall:

> "Jesus loves me, this I know,
> for the Bible tells me so.
> Little ones to Him belong;
> they are weak but He is strong.
> Yes, Jesus loves me.
> Yes, Jesus loves me.
> Yes, Jesus loves me.
> The Bible tells me so."

As I sang that song over and over, God did a miracle in my life. He changed my bitter attitude completely. Oh, I was grieved for a period of time, but not bitter. I was hurt, but not angry. God gave me a new perspective. "Ron," He said, "you are here to please Me, not people. I am causing all things to work together for good. The most important thing you need to know is that I love you. I am going to care for you in the days to follow."

I started to keep a log of all that God was doing in my life. More profound insights came to me than ever before, because God was able to meet me at a point of great personal inadequacy. He began showing me that it is all right to be emotionally low, just as it is all right to be emotionally high. That it is not a mark of spirituality; it is a mark of physiology! I encourage you to turn to God in your low points. Keep a log or a diary as you experience highs and lows in your life. Ask God to give you special insights into Him and His Word as you experience Him in your low points.[4]

S—*Seek the Lord.* This attitude of "seeking" can be illustrated by an attitude I once had, that of seeking after pastries.

A certain doughnut shop, near where I used to live in Pennsylvania, attracted me often. I became so enamored of the doughnuts that whenever I would get within a mile of that shop, I would immediately begin to visualize a hot cinammon roll with butter cascading off the sides, and I would salivate over the prospect of putting my teeth into that beautiful roll. God wants us to seek Him in that way, to go after Him with all our hearts and minds.

E—*Expect the miraculous.* We need to believe God for the miraculous development of our own character, and to trust Him for radical character transformation in the lives of people. We need to pray that God will root out blind spots and sin problems in our lives and in the lives of others.

I also need to expect the miraculous in my personal ministry. I need to ask myself regularly, "What miracle has God done in my life today or this week? What miraculous answers to prayer has God given me?" As my character changes—as I become more and more conformed to Christ—I will be able to believe God for the miraculous in my ministry.

N—*Need God.* How much do you need God? If the Holy Spirit had not been resident within you this last week, how would your life have been different? Now, really—be honest! Could you have acted the same way you acted, had the same thoughts you had without the Holy Spirit being there? What demonstration is there in your life that you need God? We need to *learn* to recognize our need for God. We need to sing the song, "I need Thee every hour," and really mean it.

If you read the histories of great men and women of God, you will find that they were men and women who had an utter dependence upon God. They said, "If God doesn't do it, it can't be done."

C – *Confess regularly.* Confession should not consist of merely recognizing the sin, but also of admitting to God that we have hurt Him, thanking Him for His unconditional love and forgiveness and then repenting or turning away from that sin.

The reality of God's forgiveness came through to me some years ago at a conference where Dr. Bill Bright asked us to write down all of our sins on a piece of paper. I thought I could write all mine down on a 3 x 5 card. But as I prayed and began writing, I filled out one and one-half sheets of paper.

Then Dr. Bright asked us to write 1 John 1:9 on that paper. So I wrote, "If we confess our sins, He is faithful and righteous to forgive us our sins and to cleanse us from all unrighteousness."

He then pointed out that we need to admit our sins once and for all, and accept the fact that God has forgiven us for all of them. Then we need to practice spiritual breathing. This unique concept calls for us to exhale spiritually when we sin. I do this by admitting that I was wrong, turning from my sin and thanking God for forgiving me. Then I inhale spiritually by asking God to control me and empower me.

I discovered that by using this principle of spiritual breathing I could live every hour experiencing and enjoying God's forgiveness. It is a fact that I will sin, but I can immediately rebound by confessing my sin, accepting God's forgiveness and continue on in my activities with a pure heart.

E – *Enjoy the Lord.* Psalms 34:8 says, "O, taste and see that the Lord is good." The implications of enjoying God carry over into our personal relationships. We need to learn to enjoy people. Everybody is unique – believers and unbelievers alike. We can enjoy God by enjoying people, reveling in our uniqueness and in our similarities. We can also enjoy God by enjoying nature – His creation. Like people, His physical creation was made to glorify Him. We too are to glorify God, and (as the Westminster catechism says) "to enjoy Him forever."

Not only do we need to love the Lord with all our mind (by meditating) and with all of our heart and soul (by enjoying the presence of God), but we need to love the Lord with all of our strength. That involves having a radical commitment to Him. ·All too often, however, our commitment is sadly lacking.

By contrast let's look for a moment at the commitment of a young convert to communism. Although I deplore many of its ideals, methods and morals, I applaud the commitment of some of its members. It's this kind of commitment that has caused communism to mushroom from a small group of 17 people in 1903 to a movement today that threatens to engulf the world. Here is part of a letter one of its adherents wrote to his fiancee:

> There is one thing I am dead earnest about and that is the communist cause. It is my life, my business, my religion, my hobby my sweetheart, my wife and my mistress, my bread and my meat. I work at it in the daytime and dream of it at night. Its hold on me grows, not lessens as time goes on. Therefore, I cannot carry on a friendship, a love affair, or even a conversation without relating it to this force which both thrives and guides my life. I evaluate people, books, ideas and actions according to how they affect the communist cause and by their attitude toward it. I have already been in jail because of my ideals and if necessary I am ready to go before a firing squad.[6]

In light of this man's commitment, ours seems shallow for the most part. Instead, the commitment of the Christian should be of the highest order because we have the greatest leader of all history and the greatest cause.

The strength of our commitment flows from our love for Christ. His words in Luke 14:26 give us insight about what our love for Christ should be like. "If anyone comes to Me, and does not hate his own father and mother and wife and children and brothers and sisters, yes, and even his own life, he cannot be My disciple."

Does this passage teach that we are to hate our brother, sister, mother, father, wife, children and even ourselves? No! Jesus is saying, "In comparison to your love for all these, your love for Me ought to be supreme, so overwhelming that the other love seems as hate." God wants a supreme, supernatural, Christ-centered love from His children.

A.W. Tozer, a great man from years past, formulated some questions we should ask ourselves. They will reveal a great deal about our commitment to Christ and how supreme our love for Him is.

What do you want the most? When everything is gone, when all the activities you have to do are done, when you are alone, what do you want more than anything else in the world? I believe Scripture tells us we should want to know Christ in the most personal, intimate, powerful way possible.

What do you think about most? You have a lot of things to think about—school, ministry, family, job. But when you are alone, what is the thing that secretly occupies your mind? Is it your reputation, the future, power, money, the ministry? Or is it the Lord?

How do you spend your money? You might spend it on a lot of things. You might even give a tenth of what you make to the Lord, but how do you spend what you have left?

What do you do with your leisure time? Everyone is busy, but when you have time to be alone, how do you spend it? Do you watch TV, listen to the radio, read, participate in sports—disproportionately? How does that use of time demonstrate the supremacy of your love for Christ.

What kind of company do you enjoy? If you could be with anybody, with whom would you choose to be and why?

Whom and what do you admire the most? Is it the qualities of Christ and the people who represent His qualities, or is it people who might have a powerful impact in the business or professional world? True, there are many good principles to follow in the business world and God is greatly using laymen in full-time secular work, but there are qualities in believers that ought to be admired even more.

These questions are convicting, aren't they? But they allow us to see some areas where we need to trust the Holy Spirit to work in our lives. God wants us to burn and glow in our commitment to Him. He wants us to love Him with all of our heart, soul, mind *and* strength.

This sounds fanatical. It is inconsistent with natural thinking. But it is people who burn with commitment, who are consumed with love for Jesus Christ and who are empowered by God's Holy Spirit, who will make an impact on families, on churches and on our world.

Action Points

1. Evaluate yourself on each of these aspects of practicing the presence of God. I do this:

P—Praise God continually	1 2 3 4 5
R—Rejoice in negative circumstances	1 2 3 4 5
E—Experience the Lord in my low points	1 2 3 4 5
S—Seek the Lord	1 2 3 4 5
E—Expect the miraculous	1 2 3 4 5
N—Need God	1 2 3 4 5
C—Confess regularly	1 2 3 4 5
E—Enjoy the Lord	1 2 3 4 5

2. Select one of these areas which need improvement in your life and ask the Holy Spirit to empower you to see change in that area in the next 30 days. Each day concentrate on this particular item and trust the Holy Spirit to work through you as you discipline yourself for the purpose of godliness.

RECOMMENDED READING

How to Succeed the Biblical Way, Ron Jenson, Tyndale House

"Have You Ever Made the Wonderful Discovery of the Spirit-Filled Life?" Bill Bright, Here's Life Publishers

The Holy Spirit: The Key to Supernatural Living, Bill Bright, Here's Life Publishers

CHAPTER FOUR

The Breakdown of the Family

> No nation, especially this one at this stage of its history, can afford to neglect its children. The welfare of our children has to be our highest priority. Not only are they our future security, but their dreams and ideals can provide a much-needed renaissance of spirit in what is becoming an aging, tired and disillusioned society. In the end, the only thing we have is our young people. If we fail them, all else is vain.—
> Allen Pifer, president of the Carnegie Corporation.

The family has experienced major breakdowns in recent years—both in the husband-wife relationship and in the parent-child relationship. One of the factors contributing to the breakdown of marriage is the promiscuous society we live in today.

Movies, television, books and magazines glamorize sex outside of marriage. But is it all it's been advertised to be? Consider a man whose story is told by Joyce Landorf in her book *Tough and Tender*:

A man I'll call George used to work at my husband's bank. George had recently been divorced and was now establishing himself as the most eligible bachelor about town. Each day the bank tellers at the bank where he was employed excitedly gossiped about his latest word, and the male officers crowded around him at lunch to hear about his most recent sexual escapade. Months went by and George seemed to be living a hysterically marvelous, enviable life. He had taken up residence in a swing-singles apartment at the beach and boasted about having sex every night (and twice on Sundays) with glorious girls. As one married banker marveled, "George really has it made."

But one afternoon George came up to my husband's desk and haltingly said, "Uh, Dick, could I talk to you about something?"

Then, as nearly as Dick can remember, this is what George related. "You know, Dick, I've really got it made. I'm free from the attachments of marriage. I've got this great pad at the beach and I go to bed with one sexy gal after another. I come and go as I please and I do my own thing. But something is really bothering me and I can't figure it out. Every morning as I get dressed for work I look into the mirror and I think, *What was last night's sexy little game all about? Sure the girl was good looking. She was good in bed and she left this morning without bugging me, but is that all there is in life?* I asked myself, 'If this life-style is what every guy thinks he wants, why am I so depressed? Why do I feel a cold nothingness all the time?' "

He stopped, leaned closer to Dick, and quietly continued. "I know the guys here think it would be fantastic to have this kind of liberated freedom but honestly, Dick, I hate this life." He sat back and paused for a few seconds and then wistfully added, "You know what I'd really like? I'd like to go home tonight, smell dinner cooking, hug my wife hello, and spend the evening telling her how much I love her. I'd like to go to bed with her and not have to prove my virility, not have to sexually perform above the call of duty, but just give her love, and go to sleep knowing she'd be there in the morning."

The trend toward extra-marital sex is reflected in the Census Bureau reports that 1.1 million unmarried male-female couples are living together, nearly double the figure reported in 1970, with the sharpest rise occurring since 1977 in the under-25 category.[1]

Social scientists believe the trend toward living together indicates an alarming loss of faith in institutions. "The real issue is not cohabitation but the meaning of marriage," says sociologist Richard Sennett. "Something about making a lifetime commitment of marriage doesn't work anymore — that's what cohabiting shows. The idea of a permanent commitment to another human being has lost its meaning."

A second factor contributing to the destruction of marriage in America is the skyrocketing divorce rate. In the last 20 years, the divorce rate has more than doubled until there is now nearly one divorce for every two marriages. The National Center of Health Statistics reported that in 1975, for the first time in our nation's history, more than one million divorces took place in a 12-month period.

But not all the divorces show up in the statistics. Many homes in America today are divided by emotional divorce. In fact, a healthy, fulfilling marriage is a rarity. Many couples live together in the same home but are emotionally divorced.

Even highly respected Christians can be married and be civil in their external relationship, but be living totally separate lives. The husband goes to work and gets involved in his activities while the wife becomes enmeshed in her own career, the lives of her children or Bible studies and other good activities. But there is no oneness; there is no unity of heart and mind in the couple. Perhaps your own marriage is drifting dangerously in this direction. Here are some symptoms:

- feelings of disillusionment, boredom, emptiness, loneliness in your marriage;
- indifference to each other's problems and interests;
- lessening of gentleness and small courtesies;
- feelings of insecurity, jealousy;
- some feelings of being better understood by others than your spouse;
- nagging;
- not enough personal communication...most conversation mechanical, surface;
- taking each other for granted;
- frequent quarrels;
- taking advantage of each other;
- insults, rudeness, sarcasm.

An outgrowth of the trend toward unhappy marriages is the occurrence of violence in homes. Sociologist Murray A. Straus says, "For any typical American citizen, rich or poor, the most dangerous place is home—from slaps to murder." Straus reckons that as many as 8 million Americans are assaulted each year by members of their own families. [2]

According to *Time*, 16 out of 100 couples in America have violent confrontations each year. Four out of 100 wives are seriously beaten each year. Three out of 100 children are kicked, beaten or punched by their parents. [3]

Feminist Movement

Another destructive force in the husband-wife relationship today involves certain elements of the feminist movement. These elements tend to demean the role of wives, mothers and homemakers. Many from this movement try to color these roles as "imprisonment."

Certainly all of us should favor equal rights for men and women. And many committed Christians are working for this type of equality through various activities, including the women's movement today. However, some leaders of the radical element of this movement are promoting unbiblical and potentially harmful emphases for the family.

For instance, consider the following statement:

> We must destroy love...Love promotes vulnerability, dependence, possessiveness, susceptibility to pain, and prevents the full development of woman's human potential by directing all her energies outward in the interest of others.

Miss Ti-Grace Atkinson, a founding member of "The Feminist" and a former president of the National Organization of Women, claims that women understand her. She seeks to eliminate sex, marriage, motherhood and love, claiming that marriage is legalized servitude, that the male-female relationship is the basis for all human oppression.[4]

The Document, a declaration of feminism, states:

> Marriage has existed for the benefit of men and has been a legally sanctioned method of control over women...the end of the institution of marriage is a necessary condition for the liberation of women. Therefore, it is important for us to encourage women to leave their husbands and not to live individually with men...we must work to destroy it (marriage).

Gloria Steinem, editor of Ms magazine, says, "By the year 2000 we will, I hope, raise our children to believe in human potential, not God."

The feminist movement has no room for God. That is rather short-sighted of them, since God created woman in the first place and since God's Word gives a high degree of honor for women.

In Jesus' day, women were looked at much like a piece of property, with the husbands having the right to divorce them at a whim (which the women could not do) and even to marry more than one wife.

During a trip through Samaria with His disciples, Jesus broke with tradition when He spoke with a Samaritan woman and asked her for a drink. First of all, Jews were not supposed to speak to Samaritans, let alone a Samaritan

woman. And she being an immoral woman at that. Most
likely, the other women would have nothing to do with
this woman, suggested by the fact that she was forced to
draw water during the hottest part of the day instead of
during the late evening.

But Jesus had more in mind than just getting a drink of
water. He was concerned that she would drink of the water
that would quench her thirst forever. That water, of
course, the water of the Spirit of God, is accessible only
through a relationship with Christ. He cared about this
woman. He cared enough to make sure she had the opportunity to know Him as her Savior. And she took hold of
that opportunity, joyfully.

The apostle Paul is another who had a high view of
women in a society that did not. During a time when
husbands had all the rights and the wives had none, Paul
admonishes husbands to "love your wives, just as Christ
also loved the church." How's that for a tall order? He's
telling husbands to love their wives with all of the
sacrificial, unconditional, accepting love that Christ has
for His Body here on earth.

The apostle Peter continues this theme when he tells
husbands to live with their wives in an understanding way
and to grant them honor as fellow-heirs of the grace of life.

Scripture does not teach us to stop women from
exerting leadership and being assertive, dynamic people.
However, the Scriptures are very clear: there is an order
that God has established which involves a husband having
primary responsibility for and authority in the home.

Homosexuality

Another key issue that is undermining marriage and the
family in our American society is homosexuality.
"Homosexual men and women are coming out of the closet
as never before to live openly," says an April 23, 1979 issue
of *Time* magazine. "They are colonizing areas of big cities
as their own turf, operating bars and even founding
churches in conservative small towns, and setting up a
nationwide network of organizations to offer counseling
and companionship to those gays — still the vast majority —
who continue to conceal their sexual orientation."

The Institute of Sex Research, founded by Alfred C. Kinsey, defines a homosexual as anyone who has had more than six sexual experiences with a member of the same gender. On that basis, the institute estimates that homosexuals constitute 10% of the U.S. population (13% of the males and 5% of the females). Of these, according to gay leaders, perhaps only 1% or so are out of the closet.

Indicative of the extremes which are often exhibited by the gay movement is this report from *The Review of the News:*

On Sunday, June 28, 1981, an estimated 50,000 homosexuals marched up Fifth Avenue in New York City. The occasion was the 12th annual Gay Pride March. In recent years the parade has taken on increasingly uglier overtones. It has become as much an anti-God, anti-religion, and anti-Catholic parade as a "Gay Pride" march.

This year the "gays" took over the steps and front of St. Patrick's Cathedral, and made it their reviewing stand. Despite the presence of large numbers of police at the scene, the Cathedral was allowed to become the focal point of the parade. With the police indifferent, there was no one to prevent the desecration of the Cathedral, now a customary feature of these demonstrations. Last year, for instance, a 20-foot banner was spread across the entrance of St. Patrick's proclaiming: "God is Gay"!

Herb McKay, a 48-year-old captain of the New York City Fire Department and a father of seven children, saw what was happening. McKay asked Cathedral officials to have the crowd removed from the steps and entrance of St. Patrick's, or at least to have the blasphemous signs and banners kept off Church property. No action was taken...

For the next two hours the parade of deviates passed by the great Cathedral. The marchers represented nearly every strata of the homosexual subculture. There were two contingents of sado-machochists dressed in black leather and chains. There was a group called the North American Man-Boy Love Association. They carried a sign declaring: Man-Boy Love Is Beautiful. Many of the "men" walked arm in arm with their "boys." Some of the youths were dressed only in bathing suits and appeared to be as young as 13.

The Gay Socialists now marched by carrying their red banners and shouting their hatred of the Church and of God. The Gay Militant Atheists stopped in front of the Cathedral and worked themselves into a frenzy, shouting: "Smash the State! Smash the Church! Death to the Church." Groups marched by chanting, "Two, four, six, eight,/ Do you know if/ Your kids are straight?" One of these gangs chanted, "Pope John Paul,/ Are you gay?" as they passed the Cathedral. Another carried a banner proclaiming: "Christ Was a Homosexual."

And so it went all afternoon. By mid-day the whole front of the great Cathedral was emblazoned with disgusting banners and provocative signs. One proclaimed: "God is Gay." A "gay flag" had been hung from the door of the Cathedral. It was designed like the American flag, but had lavender instead of red stripes, and 50 sex symbols were substituted for Old Glory's stars.

Indeed, the parade ended in Central Park where many of the participants engaged in sex acts publicly.

But that night the television coverage completely ignored the desecration and blasphemies at St. Patrick's Cathedral. Television viewers saw only shots of ordinary marching bands and "civil rights" marchers. A monstrous abomination was made to seem like a hometown Memorial Day parade. Fire Captain Herb McKay and Attorney Andrew McCauley knew better.

Some 40 Congressmen worked on sponsoring an amendment to the Civil Rights Act of 1964 that would forbid discrimination in jobs, housing, public facilities or federally aided programs on the basis of "affectational or sexual orientation," as well as race or religion.[5]

The homosexual movement is in direct conflict with biblical Christianity. The Bible clearly points out homosexuality as sin. Romans 1:26,27 talks about the results of people rejecting what they knew to be true about God:

For this reason God gave them over to degrading passions; for their women exchanged the natural function for that which is unnatural, and in the same way also the men abandoned the natural function of the woman and burned in their desire towards one another, men with men committing indecent acts and receiving in their own persons the due penalty of their error.

Though, in practice, homosexuality may appear to be a disease, the Scripture calls it sin. But, the Bible also says that people who practice this sin can be forgiven and can be delivered from its insidious grip. 1 Corinthians 6:9-11 talks about some of the early Christians having been homosexuals, idolaters, adulterers and other kinds of sinners, yet they were washed, justified and sanctified in the name of the Lord Jesus Christ. The same thing can happen today. The homosexual can be forgiven of his sin and through a total commitment of his life to Christ can have the power to be freed from enslavement.

Dan Clark was one of the homosexuals who found this to be true. Clark had left his small home town in the Midwest at the age of 20 to seek gay companionship in a large city. There he met a "lover" in a gay bar and lived with him for about a year. Suddenly, Dan's lover, Paul, left him to become involved in a Christian ministry to gays.

"I was shocked and furious," Clark recalls. "I hated Christians, and suddenly I hated him."

For several weeks Clark strove to overcome his feeling of loss and rejection. He resented the Christian group for "stealing" Paul away, but he decided to attend Paul's church, Open Door Community Church, so he could see him again. During his teens, Clark had rejected his evangelical upbringing, although he had once taught Sunday school and counseled kids at summer youth camp.

But now, the congenial group of Christians graciously welcomed Clark to their gathering. He sat nervously beside Paul as the group sang songs of praise and adoration to God. "God seemed so real among those people," Clark recalls.

"Suddenly, what they had—peace and joy—I wanted, too. Someone kindly asked me if I had ever asked Jesus Christ to come into my life. The Bible says that Jesus knocks on the door of a sinner's heart waiting to come in. That night He was pounding on the door of my heart, so I decided to turn from my sins and give my life to Him."

Shortly afterward Clark began to attend Love in Action, in Los Angeles, a Bible study for members of the church who came from homosexual backgrounds. At weekly meetings he listened as other ex-gay Christians told of their struggles and successes. Clark eventually came out of his homosexuality, married a young woman in the church and became a pastor. But his victory, like those of most ex-gay Christians, did not come easily.[6]

It is not my intention to be overly simplistic or harsh at this point. Many people today truly do struggle with homosexual desires for a variety of reasons. Many of them are confused, fearful and frustrated. They yearn for help. They need to know, however, that homosexual, lustful thoughts and practices are sinful and can be dealt with victoriously through Christ. My major point is that the seeming acceptance of homosexual practice and lifestyle, and its blatant promotion, serves to undermine the family.

A fifth key force that is undermining husband-wife relationships is the passive male syndrome. Far too many husbands have abdicated their leadership role in the family, as well as in much of the rest of society where their leadership is sorely needed. Dr. James Dobson, associate clinical professor of pediatrics at the University of Southern California, puts this critical lack of leadership in its proper perspective. He sees it not as just affecting a few homes, but our entire nation.

"If America is to survive," he says, "it will be because husbands and fathers begin to put their families at the highest level of priority and reserve something of their time, effort and energy for leadership within their own homes."

As I have pointed out some of these pitfalls for the American marriages, you might have found yourself admitting that you're at the bottom of one of those pits right now. Don't despair. God has already forgiven you of the sin that allowed you to slip into that pit. That sin might have been pre- or extramarital sex. It might be the anger that leads to involvement in the feminist movement. It might be the selfishness and building up of emotional walls that lead to divorce.

Whatever your struggle and/or sin, you can experience God's cleansing today. He promises to cleanse if we will but ask Him. Consider His promise in 1 John 1:9, "If we confess our sins, He is faithful and righteous to forgive us our sins and to cleanse us from all unrighteousness."

Once we have been forgiven of our sins, we need to commit our lives unreservedly to Christ and trust Him for His power to live our lives as He would have us to do.

Undeniably, there are problems in the family. We have looked at some of the forces that are gnawing away at marriage relationships in our nation. Now, let's examine a few of the factors that are eroding parent-child relationships.

One of the most prominent negative influences on parent-child relationships today is the ever-increasing number of divorces. The number of children involved in divorce has tripled in the last 20 years. Currently in our nation there are 12 million children under the age of 18 whose parents are divorced.

In a study of 26 children of divorced parents in Marin County, California, social worker Judith Wallerstein was struck by the children's pervasive sense of sadness.[7]

One eight-year-old girl tells of her parents' divorce:

> I remember it was near my birthday when I was going to be six that Dad said at lunch he was leaving. I tried to say, "No, Dad, don't do it," but I couldn't get my voice out. I was too much shocked. All the fun things we had done flashed right out of my head and all the bad things came in, like when he had to go to the hospital with his bad back and when he got mad at me. The bad thoughts just stuck there. My life sort of changed at that moment. Like I used to be always happy and suddenly I was sad.[8]

Around one million children each year experience divorce in their family. "The trauma of divorce is second only to death," says child psychologist Lee Salk. "Children sense a deep loss and feel they are suddenly vulnerable to forces beyond their control."

According to one census bureau expert, 45% of the children born in a given year may spend at least part of their childhood with only one parent.[9]

> In a way, I thought I'd made it happen, said one nine-year-old girl. I thought maybe I'd acted mean to my mother and sister and I was being punished by God. So I tried to be really good by not waking Mom before schooltime and getting my own breakfast and maybe God would change His mind. But it's been three years now, and I'm used to it all. Sometimes when I make a wish with an eyelash, though, I still wish for Dad to come home.[10]

Teens are affected by divorce in different ways from smaller children. According to University of Virginia psychologist E. Marvin Hetherington, who recently completed a study on 72 divorced middle-class families, boys are the harder hit. They receive less support from mothers, teachers and peers because more is expected of them. The boy may begin bullying other children, then crying when they hit back. As a result of alienating boys his own age, he turns to younger boys or little girls, learning feminine rather than masculine play patterns. A girl, on the other hand, vents her sadness by crying to get attention.[11]

Rather than sitting by and bemoaning what is happening, we Christians need to get involved in helping to alleviate such a situation perhaps in our own neighborhood or church. You might want to include a divorced woman and her children in your family outings to help give her children a male with whom to identify. You fathers might want to invite sons of divorced couples to accompany you on outings with your sons.

Obviously, children whose parents are divorced have some great needs. But current trends in our society are also making life difficult for some children whose parents are married and living together. One of these trends is the increasing flow of mothers into employment outside the home. The fastest growing segment of the work force is the 5.5 million working mothers of pre-school children. Currently 43% of married mothers with children under the age of 6 work outside the home.

Another problem that has contributed to the difficulties in the parent-child relationship is the passive male syndrome, previously referred to as undermining husband-wife relationships. One of the most obvious examples of this is the miniscule amount of time fathers spend with their children. A Cornell University study revealed that middle-class fathers estimated they spent 40 minutes daily with their small children. But when their time was actually measured, it was discovered to be only 37.7 seconds a day![12]

Obviously 37.7 seconds per day is far from enough to make the proper impact on children. Especially when you consider how crucial the father's role is in shaping the lives of his children. The father contributes heavily to the development of the following basic personality elements:

- confidence — assurance of worthiness, ability to perform as expected;
- independence — ability to make wise, constructive decisions;
- achievement orientation — the drive to establish goals;
- and put forth the effort needed to accomplish them;
- self-discipline — a frame of mind that promotes the

child's well-being and inhibits undesirable behavior;

- morality — obtaining a set of values and a lifestyle that conforms to those values;
- sex-typing — the development of wholesome attitudes toward the opposite sex.

Social scientists have discovered that the father contributes to these personality traits through countless actions and attitudes, whether or not he is aware of what he is doing.[13]

Child Abuse

A further indication of the decay of parent-child relationships is the increasing evidence of child abuse in our country. In 1972, 60,000 cases were reported.[14] Just four years later, the number reported passed the one million mark.[15] The reported cases probably represent only a fraction of the actual number.

The following cases are typical of what is happening in our nation:

> An 11-year-old boy was brought to a San Francisco hospital suffering from severe malnutrition. He weighed 44 pounds, had a body temperature of 84 degrees and was in a coma. The suspicious marks on his wrists and ankles were related to his mother's and her boy friend's immobilization of the boy for hours on end by means of handcuffs, chains and locks.

> Police found a nine-year-old girl in a closet measuring 23 by 52 inches, where she had been locked for half her life. She weighed only 20 pounds and stood less than three feet tall. Smeared with filth and scarred from parental beatings, this child had become irrevocably mentally damaged.[16]

With children being treated so cruelly, is it any wonder that child abuse is the fifth leading cause of death in chldren?

Many battered children have parents who were abused when they were children. Child abuse tends to produce child abusers. Such activity takes more forms than just physical assaulting of children. It can also take the form of physical neglect or emotional assault and neglect.

Christians would do well to ask some honest questions of themselves first before looking to the faults of others. Ask yourself, "Do I humiliate or belittle my child through verbal lashings?" A second question could be, "Do I unfavorably compare my child with someone else—a brother, sister or friend?" And finally, "Do I discipline my child out of frustration and anger?"

If you answer these questions with "yes," then perhaps you need to seek God's power to deal with them in your own life.

Dale Evans Rogers says in her book, *Hear the Children Crying:* "Even the best of us have a tendency to 'fly off the handle' emotionally. There is a lurking tiger under the skins of all of us—an emotional tiger who can be turned loose in an unguarded moment—to our lasting sorrow."

But God has offered to tame your tiger, she adds. His offer is the strength to tame that evil within. God supplies the strength to keep your hostilities in check, and He will give you this power if you ask and trust Him. Many parents also have been helped to understand their feelings by talking and praying with someone who cares.

Now that you have examined your own role as a parent, ask God to forgive you of any problem areas that He has revealed to you. Relying on His strength for victory in these areas, you are now ready to help others in dealing with child abuse. Here are some practical steps you can take.

1. *Learn all you can about biblical principles of child-rearing* through books, seminars and knowledgeable people. Also, become informed of the symptoms of an abused child (see appendix).

2. *Be alert to potential child abuse in your community.* Watch for abuse during times of family crisis. Be especially wary of parents who you know have a background of emotional or physical deprivation as children.

3. *Make friends with your neighbors.* Parents in trouble often need someone to talk to, and many of them have nobody in whom they can confide. The experts say that in some situations a friendly suggestion as to where to go for help may be all that is needed.

If abuse is suspected and friendly contact is impossible or impractical, contact a local service agency (see appendix). Don't delay! A delay could result in repeated injury or death to the child.[17]

Another growing problem in today's society is that of

runaways. Like child abuse, children running away from home reflect the crumbling of parent-child relationships.

If you are like most parents, you are convinced that your child will never run away. But according to most experts, runaways come from all kinds of families, rich and poor, well-educated and less so.

"We see every kind of kid from every kind of background hit these streets," says a sergeant in charge of the runaway unit of New York City's Police Department. "Money, social position or ethnic background simply have nothing to do with running away from home. What's more, the age is dropping. Now we're coming across 13-year-old children."

The U.S. Department of Health, Education and Welfare (HEW) estimates that from 500,000 to 1 million teenagers run away each year. Just about as many girls as boys are runaways, and a great proportion of them leave for weeks or months at a time.

Many runaway girls are raped, especially if they hitchhike. Many runaways—including girls and boys—commit crimes from sheer hunger; many more just disappear. The HEW report states that 5.6 percent of runaway children—some 56,000 youngsters—are still gone after one year. Many of these never return. Many are dead.

In one instance, three girls, one 13-year-old and two 15-year-olds, arrived at New York City's bus terminal from Baltimore. They had run away from home and expected to find jobs in the big city. Just outside the terminal they were met by a pimp who promised them work. They went with him to his hotel room and when the 13-year-old balked at becoming a prostitute, she was raped. The youngster managed to escape the next day and, disheveled and crying, was helped by a police officer. The pimp was arrested and charged with rape. The girl was reunited with her parents. Her two friends haven't been heard from since.

Some runaways become so desperate that they are actually recruited as prostitutes for New York City streets by enterprising pimps who travel to Miami, Cleveland and Minneapolis, among other places.

Boys, too, aren't immune from physical abuse, beatings and prostitution. "Young male runaways are often solicited into a homosexual racket," says a police spokesman. They are attracted by the same promises made to girls and suffer the same consequences. Physical abuse abounds. For example, 27 young boys in Houston were tortured, sexually abused and then murdered — and most were runaways.

What causes this staggering runaway problem? Experts familiar with runaways agree that major causes are (1) the breakdown of families and (2) TV. Many of the messages of the media, especially TV, make youngsters feel they can solve their problems by going somewhere else. TV glamorizes life on the streets. "Kids get the impression that no matter what action they take, as long as they act, they're better off," says a New York police sergeant. "In actuality the streets are tough and heartless."

"Kids think that $50 is a lot, mostly because at home food, clothes and shelter are furnished them without cost. Then they hit a city, broke or nearly broke," explains a caseworker. "When they can't pay for food and shelter they have to hustle drugs or themselves."

What can be done to curb the blight of runaways and child pornography? Many authorities believe that "the problem stems from the breakdown of families and that the solution must come from strengthening families and not from the law."[18]

To strengthen families, parents must be educated in parenthood. As former U.S. Commissioner of Education Sidney P. Marland, Jr. puts it, "We insist plumbers have four or five years training before they put a wrench to a pipe, yet we have no system at all for the one most important role of parenthood."[19]

Such a "system" is beginning to emerge, however, with family counseling services in churches and parent-child relationship seminars. Dr. James Dobson, for example, now has produced his lectures on the family as a seven-film series which is distributed worldwide. Distributors estimate that more than 50,000 people in the United States alone view his "Focus on the Family" films *each week*. For information on ordering these films for your community. contact your local Christian film distributor.

Make yourself available to families with potential

runaway problems in your community. You do not have to wait until your friend's teenager leaves home to help. Social workers dealing with runaways say that several warning signals usually precede a child's running away. And you don't have to be an expert to spot the signals.

"Leaving home is a drastic act for a child," says Maryland social worker Kay Tolle. "Frustrations have reached a point where an ordinary event that might otherwise be ignored triggers a huge reaction. But it's typical for a child to give some indication that things are reaching this crisis level."

1. *Severe mood changes.* When a child becomes gloomily silent after a time of bickering or complaining, he or she has probably given up trying to talk with parents.

2. *School problems.* Skipping school, cutting classes or a sudden drop in performance are other indications of mounting pressures. Parents should keep in regular contact with teachers to monitor their youngster's performance.

3. *Antisocial behavior.* Sudden or heavy use of alcohol or marijuana are other indications of a child's acting out in deeds what he'd like to put into words. Constant fights with friends or increased bickering with siblings can also camouflage desperate and explosive feelings.

It is crucial that parents be sensitive to these signals in order to help. And communication—or the lack of it—is one of the single most important aspects of the parent-child relationship. "It's a true barometer of family stress," according to experts.[20] Children who feel cared about, supported and listened to are more likely to have a smoother transition through the inevitable turbulence of the teenage years.

The family is the most basic element of societal stability. And this crucial element is in danger of crumbling. We must see a turnabout immediately.

RECOMMENDED READING (OR VIEWING)

"Focus on the Family" film series by James Dobson, Word Inc.
Hide and Seek, James Dobson, Fleming Revell
You and Your Child, Chuck Swindoll, Thomas Nelson Publishers
Attack on the Family, James Robison, Tyndale House
Our Dance Has Turned to Death, Carl Wilson, Tyndale House

Action Points

1. Commit yourself to oneness in your relationship with your spouse. Begin by asking God to reveal any attitudes or actions that His Word calls sin. Confess them first to God, then to your mate.
2. Commit yourself to master your role as a parent. You must model good parent-child behavior before you can help others.
3. Start inviting other families to your home. Seek to help these people develop good relationships between their spouses and with their children. You can do this through your own example of how you treat your mate and your children, as well as words of encouragement and guidance you share with your guests.

APPENDIX

The Signs of Child Abuse

Various researchers in cooperation with the National Center on Child Abuse and Neglect have compiled a list of signals that warn of physical and emotional abuse. This list is given below. Any single factor does not necessarily constitute abuse. Some might have legitimate explanations. If there are a number of signs that occur frequently, however, child abuse or neglect should be suspected and reported.

An abused child
— bears welts or other skin injuries.
— is often unclean; his clothes are dirty or inappropriate for the weather.
— has severely abnormal eating habits.
— exhibits extremes of behavior—is unusually aggressive or destructive, or extremely passive and withdrawn; he cries excessively or shows no response to pain or pleasure.
— is either unusually adult or overly immature in actions.
— seems unduly afraid of parents.
— is wary of physical contact and apprehensive when approached by another child (particularly one who is crying).

— begs or steals food.
— engages in frequent vandalism, sexual misconduct or use of alcohol or drugs.
— needs glasses or medical attention.
— shows severely retarded physical or mental growth.
— is often tired, without energy.

An abusing parent
— seems to trust no one.
— is reluctant to give information about the child's injuries or condition; when questioned, he is unable to explain or offers farfetched or contradictory information.
— responds inappropriately to the seriousness of the child's condition, either by overreacting (becoming hostile when questioned) or underreacting (showing little concern or awareness of the child's needs).
— is overly critical of the child; he seldom discusses the child in positive terms.
— rarely touches or looks at the child; he ignores the child's crying or reacts to it with impatience.
— expects or demands behavior beyond the child's years or abilities.
— is isolated from family supports such as friends, relatives, neighbors and community groups; he consistently fails to keep appointments and discourages social contact.
— appears to be misusing alcohol or drugs (70% of all family violence is related to alcohol abuse).
— appears to lack control; he expresses his fears over losing control.
— has a history of child abuse.
— cannot be located.

How to Find Help
If you suspect child abuse, here are some suggestions for obtaining help.

Emergency situations
In cases involving extreme violence where immediate help is needed, call the police—but only if you are absolutely certain violent acts are being committed. If you feel that you need help in dealing with a problem yourself

or that you may take out your anger or frustrations on your own child, contact Parents Anonymous. The toll-free phone number is (800) 421-0353 (outside California); or (800) 352-0386 (California only).

Also, many states have 24-hour hot lines which provide immediate services. These phone numbers can be found by looking in your phone directory. The number may be listed under Child Protection Society, Child Welfare Committee, Social Service, etc.

If you have more time

Call your doctor or pastor or one of the agencies you find listed in your phone directory (as mentioned above). Further information on the treatment and prevention of child abuse can be obtained from:

> The National Center on Child Abuse
> P. O. Box 1182, N.W.
> Washington, D.C. 20013

or from:

> The American Humane Association
> Children's Division
> P. O. Box 1266
> Denver, CO 80201

CHAPTER FIVE

Solutions for the Family

You have been given a rather distressing look at the family in today's society. Divorce is rampant; homosexuality and the feminist movement are pressuring the institution of marriage. And children bear the brunt of many of these pressures. Single-parent homes, child abuse, microscopic amount of time from fathers and children running away from home are a few of the problems that have surfaced.

But in the face of these problems, the trend can be reversed. The family — that institution established by God in the Garden of Eden — can shine again. It can shine as a picture of Christ's relationship with His bride, the church.

I believe this can happen. But in order for it to happen Christians in America need to develop and follow a strategy for renewal in the family. And that strategy needs to begin with husbands and wives committing themselves to God's plan for marriage. They need to pattern their lives after the model that has been laid down in the Scriptures.

A great deal of rhetoric has been pumped into the minds of the American public on this topic — from such sources as feminists, television, literature, books and magazines. The result of this has been that many people have accepted unbiblical pictures of the roles of the husband and wife.

Because of the confusion surrounding those roles, let's take a closer look at the biblical standard. The Bible clearly states that the man is to be the lover and the leader in the marriage relationship.

Ephesians 5:23 points out that the husband is to be the leader of his wife. "For the husband is the head of the wife, as Christ also is the head of the church, He Himself being the Savior of the body." The husband's loving leadership is to be a picture of the loving leadership that Christ gives to the church.

Instead of this loving leadership being present, perversion of leadership is occurring in homes across America.

These perversions surface in the forms of dictatorial leadership, democratic leadership and defaulting leadership.

	Dictatorial	Democratic	Defaulting
Char-acter	Expects perfection, harsh, rigid, uses temper, threatens manipulates	All equal	Finds excuse why it is difficult to assume role
Conse-quences	Wife submits to maintain peace or rebels to maintain dignity and sanity	Anarchy, Chaos civil war. Both assume other will initiate, especially in sex and spiritual matters	Wife takes over. Children with no consistent pattern will have similar marriage

The perversion of defaulting in leadership is especially prevalent today. Many men come home from work, flop in front of the television set and allow it to dominate them for the rest of the evening instead of spending time with their families. Other men are so preoccupied with their jobs that they do not spend time with their families. And still others are simply too apathetic to take leadership in their homes and again simply default from their positions of leadership in the home.

Principles of leadership

Now that we have taken a look at some of the perversions of leadership, let's look at some principles of leadership. 1 Thessalonians 2:7-12 gives us eight key principles of leadership for the husband.

1. *Disciplined life* (v. 7)
   The husband can show discipline in his family by disciplining his thought life and by being disciplined in his free time around the home. This will enable him to give himself to his wife and children, and not be totally wrapped up in the TV or newspaper.

2. *Gentle spirit* (v. 7)
   The father needs to respond to his family with tenderness and patience.

3. *Fond affection* (v. 8)

   The husband grows in fond affection for his wife as he concentrates on her. This means that he cannot allow his mind to be diverted to lustful or questionable thoughts about other women or about pornographic material. His mind must be enraptured with his wife, thus enhancing a sense of affection. The husband needs to express this affection by frequent touching, caressing and kissing his wife. The children should see this affection and recognize that the parents are in love with one another.

4. *Communicate truth* (v. 8)

   The husband needs to "impart the gospel" to his family. This includes taking the leadership in spiritual matters at home. He should see to it that his wife and children are taught biblical content, trained in how to pray, how to witness and other basic skills and that they are built up in character.

5. *Impart his life* (v. 8)

   The heart of a marriage is oneness between the husband and wife. Communication on a deep, trusting, personal level is essential to the development of one who is new in the marriage relationship. The husband should invest the quality time and effort needed for this kind of communication.

6. *Die to expectations* (v. 9)

   The apostles "worked night and day so as not to be a burden" to the brethren at Thessalonica. They did not demand reciprocal action. Neither should the husband demand reciprocal action when he acts in a proper manner. For example, don't say, "I'll lead if she submits." The husband needs to fulfill His God-ordained responsibility regardless of the response.

7. *Be an example (model)* (v. 10)

   The apostles could point to their devout, upright and blameless behavior. The husband needs to take the lead in making the family's spiritual life a priority. And when there is disharmony in the home, the husband should be the first to admit wrong. Avoid this kind of attitude: "She's wrong too and I'm not going to admit anything until she comes crawling to me for forgiveness."

8. *Encourage* (v. 11)
Like the apostles, the husband needs to encourage his family. This should be done with gentleness and affirmation, not nagging. Encouragement can be seen in three components: complimenting, expressing confidence and comforting. One way to be encouraging in your home is to make a list of 10 things your spouse does that pleases you. Give her the list and then observe her reaction.

This list may seem like a tall order for some husbands. But God supplies the power for the impossible through His Holy Spirit. By being filled with the Spirit and allowing Him to control and empower you, you will find it possible to be the kind of husband that God wants you to be.

It is interesting that the command in Ephesians 5 to "be filled with the Spirit" is located immediately preceding the passage laying down God's commands to the husband and wife. Only by depending on the power of the Holy Spirit will individuals be able to obey these commands and make their marriage all that God intended.

Husband as a lover

In addition to the husband being the leader of the family, he is also called to be the lover. Ephesians 5:25 lays out this high calling, "Husbands, love your wives, just as Christ also loved the church and gave Himself up for her."

How does Christ love the church? With a sacrificial, giving, compassionate love. As husbands, our love for our wives should be similar.

In addition the Ephesians 5 passage says: "So husbands ought also to love their wives as their own bodies." We all love our bodies, care for them and give them special consideration in times of need. Think of the last time you injured your foot, smashed a finger or strained a muscle. You probably favored that injured part of your body and did your best to nurse it back to health as soon as possible. Husbands, you should extend that same kind of care and concern to your wife. Love her sacrificially. Love her compassionately. Love her with tender concern.

1 Corinthians 13:4-7 (Phillips translation) states so beautifully what love is all about. "This love of which I speak is slow to lose patience — it looks for a way of being constructive. It is not possessive: it is never anxious to impress nor does it cherish inflated ideas of its importance.

"Love has good manners and does not pursue selfish advantage. It is not touchy. It does not keep account of evil or gloat over the wickedness of other people. On the contrary, it is glad with all good men when truth prevails. Love knows no limit to its endurance, no end to its trust, no fading of its hope; it can outlast anything."

In a phrase, love is finding a need and meeting it. For the husband, he needs to find a need in his wife and children and meet it. As an action point, I would encourage you husbands to glance over the following list of frequently expressed needs of a woman and meet just one of them today.

What does a woman need?

1. Security
2. Love
3. To express emotion
4. Companionship
5. Closeness
6. To express herself creatively
7. To express herself mentally
8. Intimacy
9. Spiritual fulfillment
10. Romance
11. Communication
12. To feel attractive
13. Encouragement
14. Appreciation
15. To be needed

The owner of a California construction company saw his life change remarkably as he began modeling the biblical role of being a leader and a lover in his family. This sturdy engineer by the name of Bob Kruse had built his company into a profitable enterprise through discipline, hard work and tough-mindedness.

Although he had a nice wife and six teenage children, his marriage was still one of his few failures. "Bob was very domineering," his wife, Trudy, explains. "And often he would stop people, especially our oldest son, with a few well-chosen words. Bob wouldn't let him finish a sentence, or he'd jump to a conclusion about what our son was trying to say."

Feeling the frustration of family problems, Bob and Trudy involved themselves in endless activities, but Trudy felt increasingly unsure and empty.

"I knew I needed a spiritual leader," says Trudy. "I was really crying out in my prayers that the Lord would reach out in His mercy and touch Bob in spite of my life-style. If Bob looked at my Christian life, I knew he would never come to the Lord, because I was such a poor example."

Trudy was unaware that Bob felt an equal amount of personal dissatisfaction. They began a search to solve these problems by renting a beach house where they could be alone and discuss where they were going.

It was during this personal retreat that Bob committed his life to Jesus Christ. "I told God that I was 40 years old, and I had a lot of water under the bridge, but from that time on I wanted to be different."

For the next three months Trudy observed Bob arising faithfully in the early morning hours for a time of Bible study and prayer.

"I can't remember ever being so miserable before," Trudy says. "All of a sudden God had given me this spiritual leader, and He was saying to my heart, 'I want you, too, Trudy.'"

When she finally relented to God's prompting, she told Him, "If You will have me in my miserable condition, then please take me, too."

As the Kruses grew in their faith and applied biblical principles in their home, changes began to take place. Bob began to relate to his children in a calmer, more attentive spirit. "I began to realize that I'd need to change my own life before I could expect my children to change," Bob said. "What the kids were really observing was a miracle in our family."

Through the example of their parents and a variety of personal experiences, the children, one by one, began to trust Christ with their lives. "This, of course, didn't solve everything," Bob said. "There have been many experiences of testing as God worked to resolve the consequences of all those years of doing my own thing."

As time passed, the Kruses did not limit their ministry just to their family. Drawing upon their experiences of using God's principles to lead their own children through the difficult teen years, they have taught and counseled high school groups. They also felt burdened for other people living in their high-income community and have organized evangelistic outreaches at their home to convey how Jesus Christ has brought a genuine success into their personal lives.[1]

The Kruse family is an example of what can happen when the husband truly becomes the leader and the lover in the home.

Husband as a Father

In addition to being the lover and the leader for his wife, the husband needs to be a good father to his children. One little fellow, frightened by lightning and thunder, called out one dark night, "Daddy, come. I'm scared."

"Son," the father said, "God loves you and He'll take care of you."

"I know God loves me," the boy replied. "But right now I want somebody who has skin on."[2]

Fathers need to be God with skin on for their children. Not that they can be perfect, but they need to model godly characteristics for the little watchers in their home.

The Effective Father points out that family life is like a classroom. "Within the classroom are children who are like large lumps of clay," says author Gordon MacDonald. "The longer they live, the harder the clay will become unless the potter (you, the father) consciously sustains the molding process, keeping the clay pliable—shapable."

But how can a dad find opportunities to be the kind of teacher who helps shape good attitudes and actions in his children? Here are some suggestions:

1. Read to your preschooler.

2. As he grows, maintain a pattern of learning together by reading books of common interest. Discuss together newspaper articles or television news.

3. Praise your children's accomplishments and help them to understand what they can do to overcome weaknesses.

4. You probably have all kinds of educational experiences available to you — camping trips, outings to the
library, tours of museums and historical sites, festivals,
fairs and community events. Take family outings to some
of these locations.

5. With pressured time schedules so prevalent, perhaps
you could incorporate time with your children into activities you already do. Such things as driving across town
on an errand, working around the house, going shopping or
exercising provide excellent opportunities for informal
communication. Such non-threatening settings can result
in honest discussions. Ask good questions, and make sure
you are listening to the answers. Develop the habit of
looking your child in the eye. Work hard at understanding
what he is saying and feeling.[3]

Henry Biller and Dennis Meredith in their book *Father
Power* give a case study of two high school boys named
Ralph and Jimmy who demonstrate the fact that fathers
should spend quality time with their children and reinforce
proper values.

Ralph was popular at parties, an accomplished football
player and a sought-after friend by the other boys. Jimmy,
however, was not a very popular boy in high school. He
also enjoyed a close circle of friends but was more interested in debating and the math club than in athletics.
He acted in the class play and played the flute in the band.

Ralph and Jimmy both had about the same grades in
high school and had fathers who were very successful and
respected. However, a major difference between them was
their relationship with their fathers. Ralph's father was
proud of his son and often rooted for him at football games
but didn't see much of him otherwise. He taught his son
that men were strong and aggressive but left it at that.

Jimmy's father spent time learning about Jimmy's
activities, going places with him, and simply talking with
him about a variety of subjects. He taught his son that
masculinity was a complex thing to be worked out by each
person individually and that Jimmy should have confidence in what he felt was masculine.

Though Ralph was more successful socially in high

school than Jimmy, when these two boys went out into the world, there was an abrupt reversal. Ralph took a few semesters of college and dropped out. After basking in the glories of high school, he felt ignored in the larger world of college. Because he thought being a man meant being tough and nonintellectual, he didn't care about academic work. He became a sour man, believing that the world was out of step with what he thought it should be.

On the other hand, Jimmy blossomed. After four years of hard work at college, during which he also went out for the soccer team, Jimmy went on to law school and ended up as a public defender.

This is not to say that being in the math club is superior to being on the football team. But, as the authors state, "The difference in these two boys was in how their fathers had taught them to think about being competent men. Regardless of how outwardly successful a boy or girl may be, if he isn't taught what competence as a male or female really means, he is likely to end up very unhappy."

Once again, this emphasizes the father's need to spend quality time with his children and begin to implant in those children the values that will equip them to deal effectively with the outside world and have a healthy self-concept.

This is not an easy task. It takes a lot of hard work for fathers to keep the home a priority. This is certainly true for me. I have a typical executive lifestyle which involves traveling a good deal of the time. Working long hours, I'm devoted to my job and to my ministry. However, God has called me to love my wife and my children above my ministry. If my family is not a priority, I will never be as effective for the cause of Christ as I should be.

Role of the Wife

Now that we have touched on the man's role as husband and father, let's examine what the wife can do to strengthen her family.

Obviously, men and women are different physiologically. Not so readily, apparent, however, is the difference in their psychological and emotional makeup.

The Bible takes into account these differences and describes correspondingly different roles for the marriage relationship.

Earlier, we saw that the man was to lead and to love. The Bible calls the woman to submit and to help.

We looked at Ephesians 5 earlier and how it outlines the man's responsibility to love and to lead his wife as Christ does the church. This same passage has guidelines for the woman's role. It begins by admonishing all believers to "be subject to one another in the fear of Christ."

Verses 22 and 24 give some specific direction for wives. "Wives be subject to your own husbands, as to the Lord.... But as the church is subject to Christ, so also the wives ought to be to their husbands in everything."

This theme is elaborated on in 1 Peter 3:1: "In the same way, you wives, be submissive to your own husbands so that even if any of them are disobedient to the word, they may be won without a word as they observe your chaste and respectful behavior."

Many women today have problems with the word "submission" and "be subject to." They think this means enslavement. I'd like to propose a definition of submission: the yielded, intelligent, humble obedience to an ordained authority. Christ was the ultimate example of submission. Throughout His time on earth, He submitted Himself to the will of the Father.

In the Garden of Gethsemane, He prayed fervently to the Father to "remove this cup from Me." He did not want to go through the agony of the cross and the resulting separation from His Father in heaven. But He continued His prayer with these words, "Yet not what I will, but what Thou wilt."[4] Christ's example of submission was yielded, intelligent (He dialogued with the Father about the decision to go to the cross), and showed humble obedience to an ordained authority (in this case, God the Father).

The reason submission is so strategic in the male-female relationship is that man's greatest need is for respect. The way that a man can be hurt the most is by being rejected publicly or privately by his wife. Husbands may act like they're tough, but inside they tend to be very sensitive to their wife's respect, or lack of respect, for them.

What are some of the practical ways you, as a wife, can submit to your husband? Don't put him down. Don't react to your husband's decisions: instead respond to them. Be patient with his leadership. Don't push him into a mold. Cultivate a grateful spirit. Build loyalty in the children and in yourself to your husband. Encourage him. Allow him to lead.

Another key item for women to remember in submitting to their husbands is to forgive and forget when your husband has wronged you. When we truly forgive and forget, the following things happen:

1) We don't dwell on the problem.
2) We never bring it up to the individual again.
3) We never bring it up to anybody else.

One final point about submitting: act and look like a lady. My wife models this characteristic beautifully. Molly is a multi-talented woman with strong leadership capabilities, yet she submits to me in the most appropriate way. So submitting does not mean that you have to negate all of the gifts and talents God has given you.

In addition to submitting to their husbands, wives are to be a helpmate to their husbands. Unfortunately, many wives seem dedicated to tearing down their mates instead of building them up. One wife said, "Everybody else tells him how wonderful he is. Somebody needs to keep his head small!"

Her criticism and antagonism helped drive her husband toward another woman. In confidential session he told a counselor, "I want to be important only to her, but it seems that nothing I do pleases her." He didn't love the woman with whom he was having an affair, but he felt like a failure at home.[5]

This concept of the wife as a helpmate to her husband is outlined in the second chapter of Genesis. After creating the heavens and the earth, vegetation and animals, God created man and placed him in the Garden of Eden. Although man was in a perfect environment (no smog or pollution there!) and was in perfect harmony with God, the

Creator said, "It is not good for the man to be alone; I will make him a helper suitable for him."

So man was incomplete without a helpmate. And when God met that need by creating a helpmate suitable for Adam, he was ecstatic. A modern paraphrase of his words might be something like this: "Wow! Where have you been all my life?"

Eve was able to complete her husband, Adam, even as wives of today can bring a degree of completeness to their husbands that is not possible for them to attain as a single person. A wife can complete what is lacking in her husband, so that together they may more perfectly reflect the image of Jesus Christ to the world.

Here are some ideas on how a wife can complete her husband by being a helpmate:

- Make your husband your number one ministry and concern. Make the atmosphere of your home one of encouragement, assurance, affection.
- Be content and industrious in areas of responsibilty (Proverbs 31).
- Be sensitive to your husband's needs.
- Let him know that he has the freedom to fail—as a husband, father, or provider—and you will still love and accept him.

In addition to their calling to their husbands, women also have numerous responsibilities to their children. Some feminists would have us believe that any woman who stays at home to help raise her children is opting for a dead-end lifestyle. They feel that children are a problem at best, or a curse to be avoided at all costs. Some even advocate murdering the unborn through abortion so children will not hinder a woman's career.

The Bible gives a radically different perspective. Psalms 127:3 says, "Behold, children are a gift of the Lord; the fruit of the womb is a reward." The Bible views children as a gift, not a problem; a reward, not a curse.

Women can have an activist, leadership role in society, but when they have children, that needs to be their primary concern. My concern is that Christian women are putting their children in day-care centers day after day and week after week while they pursue their own goals.

For some women, this is necessary in order for them to survive financially in our society. But too often, Christian women have allowed the world to push them into its mold. They have allowed themselves to believe the lie that only a job outside the home has real significance. Many women today do not see mothering as the high calling it really is — a position of tremendous influence. It involves shaping the lives of those who will shape the world in the next generation.

Consider the example of a woman by the name of Susannah Annesley Wesley. Married at the age of 19 to a Church of England clergyman, she gave birth to 19 children in the next 21 years. In addition to assisting in the religious instruction of her children, Susannah tutored them in reading, writing, grammar and arithmetic. It was also her custom to set aside a certain time weekly for the religious instruction of each child.

Susannah's 15th child, born in 1703, absorbed his early education at home quickly and later went on to Oxford for his schooling. In the years to come that child, John Wesley, was the spark of the Great Awakening that inflamed England, resulting in countless changed lives and renewed social consciences.

John's younger brother, Charles, was to become the poet and hymn writer of the great evangelistic movement. Without question, Susannah Annesley Wesley had influenced the world through her offspring. Motherhood had been a high calling to her. And her dedication to this calling resulted in blessing for her entire nation.

Family Renewal

Becoming good mothers, fathers, husbands and wives is how we can bring about renewal in the families of America today. As we model the biblical role for husbands and wives we will create a thirst in other people to experience the fruit of a godly family relationship. Also, we should be quick to share the biblical principles of marriage with others. Frequently an unhappy home life can point an individual to his need for the ultimate head of a home — Jesus Christ.

We also need to evangelize people of influence in this

strategic area. Make a list of people in your community who are involved in women's liberation, gay liberation and other anti-family causes. We can't see these leaders just as the "bad guys," but as people who need Christ. Seek to reach them with the gospel through personal contact or by reaching their friends.

We need to speak out against the immorality we see in the family. Concerned Women for America and other groups are very much involved in this. Get their newsletters and communications from other similar groups so you can be informed and take part in making your voice heard on a national level as well as in your home area.

We need to see fundamental moral change in America's families. Let's continue to model biblical roles, evangelize and speak out until we do see change in this essential institution.

Action Points

1. If you are a husband, consider the role you have in your family. Does your leadership style fall into the pattern of dictatorial, democratic, or defaulting (see chart on p. 70)? If so, determine how you will correct your style to bring it into line with the biblical pattern.
2. Review the list of women's needs on page 73. Determine to help meet just one of those needs today.
3. If you are a wife, determine a way you can build up your husband and commit yourself to doing it today.
4. If you feel your spouse has wronged you in some way, forgive and *forget*. This means not to dwell on the problem once it has been dealt with and not to bring it up again to your spouse or anyone else.

CHAPTER SIX

Abortion, Infanticide, and Euthanasia

What we face today is a sort of "domino principle," in which certain people are being reclassified as nonpersons. First it's the unborn child, with abortion; then infanticide follows, and finally the elderly are set aside. Abortion is not the only issue. The basic issue is the concept that there is such a thing as human life not worthy to be lived.[1]—Jim Buchfuehrer

While the family is being assaulted through the breakdown in the relationship between hubands and wives as well as in the breakdown between children and parents, there is an equally dangerous assault in the form of legalized murder: abortion, infanticide and euthanasia. These are outright attacks on basic human worth. In my mind, this springs from the concept of evolution which says that people are evolved from animals anyway, so they're not really worth much. This is a faulty view of man because, according to the Scriptures, man is made in the image of God.

Abortion

The most prominent of these attacks on human worth is abortion. In 1973, the Supreme Court declared that a new personal right or liberty existed in the Constitution — the right of a woman to procure an abortion at any time.[2]

Since that decision, the number of legal abortions has increased considerably, from 899,000 in 1974 to about 1.3 million in 1977.[3] One-third of these abortions were obtained by teenagers and three of four performed·on unmarried women.[4]

In Washington, D.C., the number of legal abortions obtained by Washington residents has exceeded the number of births for the first time. The Department of Human Resources said about 85% of the abortions had been paid for by the government.

Some 76% of the poor women seeking abortions have had them paid for through state funds.[5] Personally I am outraged by the use of tax money for an act that I believe is morally, ethically and spiritually wrong. To me abortion is murder and this view can be supported from Scripture.

The Psalmist says in Psalms 139:13, 16: "For Thou didst form my inward parts; thou didst weave me in my mother's womb...Thine eyes have seen my unformed substance; and in Thy book they were all written, the days that were ordained for me, *when as yet there was not one of them*" (italics mine).

From this passage, we can see that the fetus is described as having its entire life planned out for it. There is no difference in God's sight between murdering a 5-year-old child and murdering an unborn child—both are living beings.

The widespread practice of abortion today illustrates how far our society has gone from scriptural standards. The U.S. Supreme Court has aided this departure by now ruling that a wife need not have her husband's consent to obtain an abortion, and unmarried teenagers no longer need parental approval to obtain an abortion.

Now it is possible for doctors to determine the sex of a fetus through a test known as amniocentesis. On the basis of this test, some patients are choosing abortion to avoid having an unwanted boy or girl. Some doctors say that the preference most often is for a boy.

Our society has a strange, convoluted set of values. It protects the seal, the whale, the otter and the whooping crane, then allows millions of unborn babies to be killed. Our society now allows parents to abort simply because they might not like the sex of the child.

The advocates of abortion like to refer to themselves as "pro-choice" rather than pro-abortion. They see themselves as championing a woman's right to choose whether or not to have a child. What they are championing, in reality, is the murder of living things.

Nowhere is this more evident than in the operating room where the abortions are done. Three commonly used techniques end early pregnancies. The most frequent is the D & C or dilation and curettage. In this procedure the cervix is stretched to permit the insertion of a curette, a tiny hoelike instrument. The surgeon then scrapes the wall of the uterus, cutting the baby's body to pieces and scraping the placenta from its attachments on the uterine wall. Bleeding is profuse.

An alternate method which is used is the suction abortion. A powerful suction tube is utilized in this method to tear apart the body of the developing baby and the placenta, sucking the pieces into a jar. Arms, legs, head and other parts of the body are recognizable at this point.

Later in the pregnancy, when the D & C or suction abortion might produce too much bleeding, doctors frequently use the saline abortion technique. This method employs a long needle being inserted through the mother's abdomen directly into the amniotic fluid which has accumulated in the sac around the baby. The salt solution is absorbed by the baby, burning off the outer layer of skin. It takes about an hour to kill the baby by this slow method. The mother usually goes into labor about a day later and delivers a dead, shriveled baby.

If abortion is decided on too late to be accomplished by the other methods, doctors resort to a hysterotomy. This is exactly the same procedure as a Caesarean section, except it is used to kill the baby rather than to save it. Babies delivered by this method are truly alive, but they are allowed to die through neglect or sometimes killed by a direct act.[6]

What can be done to help stop this form of legalized murder? Hospital personnel at Indio (California) Community Hospital managed to block some abortions by refusing to participate in them. Fifty-two nurses and aides, one-third of the nursing staff, signed a petition saying they will not participate in any more saline abortions there. The hospital was the scene of a late-term abortion by the saline method in which an infant girl was born alive, only to die 10 days later after being flown by helicopter to another hospital.

The hospital administrator said that the nurses' action had caused a temporary halt in those abortions induced by the injection of saline after the 16th week. The nurses' refusal included physical care, emotional support and administration of medicine or other treatment.[7]

In a somewhat similar situation, the nurses and medical staff at
Hollywood's Memorial Hospital (Florida) rebelled after several live
fetuses were born during second-trimester abortions. Hospital
administrator Sal Mudano commented, "We've had preemies that
have lived that were less developed than some of these abortions
were. Our personnel are not in favor of working in that kind of
situation, and the law says we can't force people to participate
against their personal or religious beliefs. It's not that we're
preaching, and we don't have a bunch of religious fanatics on our
staff. But our nurses are geared to saving lives and this is just the
opposite."[8]

Infanticide

A second force attacking human worth and the family is
infanticide. While abortion deals with the killing of an
unborn child, infanticide is the killing of children already
born. It is usually accomplished through a direct act or
through the neglect of ordinary care, such as feeding,
which is vital to the survival of the child.

Although statistics documenting the widespread
practice of infanticide in hospitals are difficult to obtain,
the *New England Journal of Medicine* reported that Yale
University's principal hospital allowed 14% of the babies in
its intensive care unit to die by withdrawing or denying
treatment because their prognosis appeared hopeless.

Dr. C. Everett Koop, former surgeon-in-chief at
Children's Hospital in Philadelphia, now U.S. Surgeon
General, was involved in the writing of a book and the
production of a film series that covered the subjects of
abortion, euthanasia and infanticide. On numerous occasions he visited with medical personnel who indicated to
him that the practice of infanticide was far wider than he
had thought.

In *An Action Alternative Handbook for Whatever
Happened to the Human Race?* Dr. Koop cites two
examples:

In one large Midwestern city, a nurse came to us after the film on
infanticide and said that she was convinced it was not true,
because she practiced in a large hospital, worked on a ward for
infants, and never heard of such a thing happening. On the night
shift Sunday night, she went to take care of one of her patients and
found a sign on the foot of the bed, saying, "Nothing by mouth: No
food, no fluids, no medicines." When she ran out to see the head

nurse, to ask what in the world was going on, the nurse replied to her in words similar to this: "Don't worry about it. It happens all the time. The parents decided they did not want the child. But don't be concerned; you're covered."

Another neonatal-intensive-care nurse came to me in some distress, telling me that in the previous several weeks, the following instances had taken place in her unit. First, after she had adjusted an intravenous in a scalp vein in an infant's head, the resident came by and knocked it out with the comment, "Don't you know that we want this baby to die?" Second, she was reprimanded for aspirating mucous out of the windpipe of a newborn. The resident told her they wanted the youngster to remain in his state of poor oxygenation because they did not want him to live.

The morals of our society have deteriorated to such an extent that infanticide has become an accepted practice. This was indicated by the Sonoma (California) Conference on Ethical Issues in Neonatal Intensive Care. At the conference, 17 members of a panel of 20 answered *yes* to this question: "Would it be right to directly intervene to kill a self-sustaining infant?" (A self-sustaining infant is a child who can live without assistance of any kind, other than normal feeding).[9]

Doctors today justify allowing children to die with a view that it saves the families crushing burdens and the child itself of a life not worth living. Yet disability and unhappiness do not necessarily go together. Some of the most unhappy children are in perfect health, while some of the happiest children have physical problems which most of us would find very difficult to endure.

A number of people who had disabling birth defects were asked about the joy of living. The patients ranged in age from 11 to 30 years old. One patient had been born with a number of major congenital defects down the midline of his body, requiring 27 operative procedures for correction. Another was born with major defects of the esophagus, the lower bowel and the bladder. Here are a few of their statements:

"Because the start was a little abnormal, it doesn't mean you're going to finish that way. I'm a normal, functioning human being, capable of doing anything anyone else can..."

"At times it got very hard, but life is certainly worth living. I married a wonderful guy and I'm just so happy..."

"At the beginning it was a little difficult going back to school after surgery, but then things started looking up, with a little perseverance and support. I am an anesthetist and I'm happily married. Things are going great for me..."

"If anything, I think I've had an added quality to my life—an appreciation of life. I look forward to every single morning."

"Most of the problems are what my parents went through with the surgery. I've been teaching high school now for eight years and it's a great joy..."[10]

Should these people have been allowed to die shortly after birth? Hasn't their life attained some sort of meaning for them? If we decide to allow children with certain defects to die, what is to prevent us from allowing adults with defects to die? They may be much more of a burden to their families than a child with a birth defect. Are we to extend the slaughter to all those who in one way or another become a burden or a nuisance, or who stop us from enjoying our rights?

Euthanasia

A society with such a low view of human worth that it allows babies to be killed inside the womb or shortly after leaving the womb will have little trouble justifying the killing of older adults—especially those who are judged unwanted, imperfect or considered a possible social nuisance.

The next candidates for arbitrary reclassification as nonpersons are the elderly. This will be increasingly true as the proportion of the old and weak becomes larger than the number of the young and strong. Many of the young will see the old as a nuisance in the pleasure-seeking lifestyle they claim as their right. As they continue to clamor for affluence, it is doubtful that the legislature and the courts will have any more compassion for the elderly than they have for the unborn and newborn.

This can be seen in some cases that have already taken place. In one situation, a Washington, D.C., grand jury refused to indict a woman who confessed to entering the hospital room of her father in order to terminate his life.

She had concealed a pair of scissors in her purse and cut the tubes providing oxygen and intravenous fluids. After his death, she presented a two-page confession, but the jury refused to bring her to trial, since the man was expected to die anyway.[11]

In another case, murder charges brought against a nurse who killed four patients — by disconnecting their respirators in the intensive-care unit of the hospital where she worked — were dropped by the Baltimore prosecutors.[12]

The philosophy of euthanasia advocates is expressed by Professor O. Ruth Russell in the February 14, 1972 issue of *The New York Times:* "Surely it is time to ask why thousands of dying, incurable and senile persons are being kept alive — sometimes by massive blood transfusions, intravenous feedings, artificial respiration and other heroic measures — who unmistakably want to die."

The statement or implication that many of these people unmistakably want to die is open to debate. On the contrary, Dr. Phillip H. Addison, who was secretary of the Medical Defense Union in London, the British Medical Association Board of Science and Education, said that dying patients seldom ask for euthanasia. Those who know they are dying usually welcome any prolongation of life.[13]

What can happen in a society that embraces euthanasia is demonstrated in the example of Nazi Germany. Long before Hitler wrote *Mein Kampf,* a book was published that advocated the elimination of a class of people. The book was written by Alfred Hoche, one of Germany's most prestigious professors of psychiatry, and lawyer Carl Binding. Their writings presented the view that many psychiatric patients were mentally dead and only partial Germans. They called for their medical murder, to relieve their suffering, to purify the race and to save the state money.

The German physicians were very cooperative when a program like this actually went into effect under Hitler. Their cooperation involved the mass extermination of the chronically sick in the interest of saving "useless" expenses to the community as a whole; the mass extermination of those considered socially disturbing or racially and ideologically unwanted; the individual, inconspicuous extermination of those considered disloyal within the ruling group; and the ruthless use of human experimental material for medico-military research.

Hitler exterminated some 275,000 people in his "killing centers." The methods used and the personnel trained in the killing centers for the chronically sick became the nucleus of much larger centers in the East, where the plan was to kill all Jews and Poles and to cut down the Russian population by 30 million.

The first to be killed were the aged, the infirm, the senile, the mentally retarded, and defective children. Eventually, as World War II approached, the doomed undesirables included epileptics, World War I amputees, children with badly modeled ears, and even bed-wetters.[14]

This incredible destruction of life all began with the acceptance of the attitude that there is such a thing as a life not worthy to be lived. They had a very low estimation of human worth. This is exactly what is happening today in abortion, infanticide and euthanasia. What happened in Nazi Germany can happen here!

Genetic Engineering

Related to the drive to destroy the family through such means as abortion, infanticide and euthanasia are the test-tube baby methods and genetic engineering that are making great strides today. In a *Brave New World* type of approach, people using these methods are seeking to oust the family by actually creating life in a test tube.

The test-tube-baby method involves the surgical removal of the egg of a female (only $\frac{1}{1000}$ of an inch long) and the fertilization of the egg with the sperm. This process takes place in a petri dish (a small covered saucer) containing a medium similar to the environment inside the fallopian tube where conception normally takes place. After a period of incubation, the fertilized egg is inserted into the uterus. The egg can then mature into a full-grown healthy fetus in the same way as a normal pregnancy.

Dr. Jean Rostand, the French biologist, commented on the advent of the test-tube babies, "It will be little more than a game to change the subject's sex, the color of its eyes, the general proportions of body and limbs, and perhaps the facial features. The man-farming biologist," he added, "might be tempted to tamper with the intellectual makeup of the subject, predetermining the behavior and attitudes of an individual for a lifetime."[15]

Genetic engineering also has some frightening implications. This field includes *in vitro* fertilization (the egg and sperm being united in the laboratory), molecular genetics, genetic counseling, medical genetics, eugenics (improvement of the quality of a race), and cloning (the biological manufacture of a human being to desired specifications).[16]

The cloning procedure involves the removal of an egg, substituting the desired nucleus (perhaps large numbers of eggs and nuclei, thus producing large numbers of individuals with exactly the same characteristics), culturing the new individuals in artificial uteri, and then harvesting the new crop of identical human beings.[17]

The feasibility of making deliberate genetic changes and manufacturing people is potentially one of the most important concepts in the history of the human race. Now the value of human worth can be reduced to just another experiment in the laboratory.

What To Do Now

With issues like genetic engineering, test-tube babies, abortion, infanticide and euthanasia pressing in on us, it would be easy to respond by throwing up our hands in despair. This is not what I believe God would have us do.

Proverbs 24:11 (NIV) says, "Rescue those being led away to death; hold back those staggering toward slaughter. If you say, 'But we knew nothing about this,' does not he who weighs the heart perceive it? Does not he who guards your life know it? Will not he repay each person according to what he has done?"

Dr. Francis Schaeffer, eminent theologian and co-author of the book *Whatever Happened to the Human Race?*, describes the need of the individual and the church to become involved in helping to meet the needs of people faced with the questions of abortion, infanticide and euthanasia:

When the married woman is facing the problem of not being able to care for an extra child, the church should share in the burden by providing an alternative, through people in the church sharing that burden with their time and, if needed, with their money.

When the unmarried woman of any age faces the question of abortion, she should know that, though the church will say she has been wrong in having sexual intercourse outside of marriage, it will have compassion in the most practical ways. This includes helping her have the child adopted into a Christian family or helping her with the practical realities of keeping the child.

The same is true with infanticide. Keeping a handicapped child has very real problems, financially and otherwise. The church should be set up for people to step in and help carry the burden.

When an old person comes to the point of needing special care and the family is being pressed by the surrounding thought forms toward euthanasia, then the church must again function. People must be willing to share their time, as well as money, to give help as a church, but also as Christian individuals.[18]

The fight against abortion has gained momentum lately. Some anti-abortionists took action by staging sit-ins at selected abortion clinics in St. Louis. Others stationed themselves at the Women's Clinical Group in that city and tried to talk arriving women out of having abortions. Ann O'Donnell, one of the pro-life leaders, believes at least one woman is dissuaded from an abortion each week through this type of effort.[19]

Become involved in helping to resolve the issues of abortion, infanticide and euthanasia in your community, state and even on the national level. See the appendix in the back of this book for a list of materials that you can obtain to become better informed about these issues. Get in touch with one of the pro-life groups currently active to see what you can do to help influence government leaders on the subject of abortion. Write letters to those in positions of authority with regard to these issues. And get others involved with you.

But be sure to pray that God's power would be released in the Christians of this country to take action in these areas. Otherwise, God's judgment is sure to come on a land which is permitting legalized murder to take place.

Action Points

1. Become better informed about these issues so that you can clearly articulate your position on abortion, infanticide and euthanasia.
2. Think of actions that you can take to help halt the growth of these three vicious attacks on the family.
3. Determine to begin acting on one of your solution steps this week.

RECOMMENDED READING

Whatever Happened to the Human Race? Francis Schaeffer and C. Everett Koop, Fleming Revell
Plan for Action: An Action Alternative for Whatever Happened to the Human Race? Fleming Revell

APPENDIX

(Editor's note: The following material is taken from *Plan for Action: an Action Alternative for Whatever Happened to the Human Race?* p. 92-95. It is an excellent guide for the person who wants information and who would like to get involved in the fight against abortion, euthanasia and infanticide.)

Pro-Life Groups

Immediately apparent to anyone in touch with the pro-life movement is the fact that one is dealing with a tremendously vital grass-roots effort. The contrast could not be greater. Planned Parenthood, which is funded annually by *millions* of tax dollars, spearheads the abortion drive. For every Planned Parenthood clinic, there is a dedicated group of people, sometimes marching under several banners, usually putting out one or more newsletters of varying originality and sophistication.

Naturally, seven years beyond the Supreme Court decision, most local groups have become affiliated with, or are dependent upon, larger groupings, which may also lobby in Washington and in state capitals. Naturally, too, most local newsletters derive some of their content and know-how from a few national newsletters. The listing below includes representative major organizations most of which issue newsletters that are available on request, along with details of local chapters. In a few special cases, the title of a newsletter is also given in the listing.

GENERAL

These groups do not specialize in any one activity, even if their output in a certain area may match that of a specializing organization.

Ad Hoc Committee In Defense of Life: 8810 National Press Building, Washington, D.C. 20045

American Citizens Concerned for Life: 6127 Excelsior Blvd., Minneapolis, MN 55416

Christian Action Council: 788 National Press Bldg., Washington, D.C. 20045. An an avowed evangelical organization, the CAC exposes the myth that abortion is a "Catholic" issue. Newsletter: *Action Line.*

Feminists for Life: P. O. Box 5361, Columbus, OH 43221. Feminism does not have to follow the abortion line.

National Right to Life Committee: 341 National Press Bldg., Washington D. C. 20045. Through its systematic organization of support across the country, RTL has become synonymous with the pro-life stand in the eyes of the public. Its Voter Survey Project is currently providing the most effective means of telling elected officials that pro-lifers mean business. In most localities, the fastest way to get in touch with the issues is to call the local RTL office. National RTL News is available from: P. O. Box 417, Wilmette, IL 60091.

National Youth Pro-Life Coalition: 235 Massachusetts Ave., NE, Washington, D.C. 20002.

Right to Life Crusade: P. O. Box 2703, Tulsa, OK 74101. Identified with Dr. Mildred Jefferson.

Right to Life of Greater Cincinnati: P. O. Box 24073, Cincinnati, OH 45224. A local chapter of RTL, but a special one, as the home ground of Dr. and Mrs. Willke, preeminent pro-life leaders. Especially good local newsletter.

United States Coalition for Life: Export, PA 15632

POLITICAL

The basic political hope of the pro-life movement is a constitutional convention, to vote an amendment to negate the Supreme Court abortion ruling.

Americans for a Constitutional Convention: 825 National Press Bldg., Washington, D.C. 20045. Publishes *The Convention Call.*

American Life Lobby: 357B National Press Bldg., Washington, D.C. 20045.

Life Amendment Political Action Committee: P. O. Box 14263, Ben Franklin Station, Washington, D.C. 20044. Very influential.

National Committee for a Human Life Amendment: 1707 "L" Street, NW. Ste. 400, Washington, D.C. 20036. Affiliated with United States Catholic Conference.

National March of Life: P. O. Box 2950, Washington, D.C. 20013. Organizes the greatest visible repudiation of the Supreme Court ruling on its anniversary each year (January 22) in Washington. Largest annual march in history — media or no media.

PROFESSIONAL/DENOMINATIONAL

American Association of Pro-Life Obstetricians and Gynecologists: 266 Pine Ave., Lauderdale-by-the-Sea, FL 33303

Baptists for Life: P. O. Box 394, Hallettsville, TX 77964.

Catholic League for Religious and Civil Rights: 1100 W. Wells St., Milwaukee, WI 53233. The first declared goal is right-to-life for unborn, aged and handicapped.

Clergy Concerned for Life: P. O. Box 411083, Chicago, IL 60641.

Lutherans for Life: 275 N. Syndicate, Box 988, St. Paul, MN 55104. Have developed an excellent presentation called Doublespeak.

Nurses for Life: P. O. Box 4818, Detroit, MI 48219. Extensive organization; valuable newsletter.

ADVOCACY

Americans United for Life: 230 N. Michigan Ave., Ste. 515, Chicago, IL 60601. Excellent intellectual, legal and medical advocacy. Apart from a general newsletter, its publication *Lex Vitae* gives up-to-date information on legal cases tried and pending. The AUL is a sort of pro-life ACLU, providing legal counsel and managing a legal-defense fund. It recently convened the First Conference on the Psychology of Abortion, whose proceedings were edited by Mall and Watts (see "Specialized Material").

Human Life Center: St. John's University, Collegeville, MN 56321. Covers whole range of life issues under direction of Dr. Paul Marx.

COMPASSION

Alternatives to Abortion International: Ste. 511, Hillcrest Hotel, Toledo, OH 43699. This grew out of the initiative of Birthright, but acts as an umbrella organization coordinating the impressively widespread efforts to give discreet help and counsel for crisis pregnancies.

Bethany Christian Services: 901 Eastern N.E., Grand Rapids, MI 49503. Adoption, residential care, foster-family care, pregnancy counseling.

Birthright: National office—"Summerhill," 62 Hunter St., Woodbury, NJ 08096. International office—761 Coxwell Ave., Toronto, Canada. Pioneer crisis pregnancy service with over 359 branches in the United States. Began as a telephone lifeline in 1968 when Louise Summerhill, its executive director, was shocked into action on a visit to London, England, by the availability of a telephone facilitating abortions.

Christian Family Renewal: P. O. Box 73, Clovis, CA 93613. Runs a "National Pregnancy Hotline.": (800) 344-7211.

Evangelical Adoption and Family Service: 201 S. Main Street, North Syracuse, N.Y. 13212. In this abortion area, such agencies have a regional profile, attracting hopeful couples from a wide area.

CHAPTER SEVEN

Religion in American Society

Since the birth of this nation, religion has played an influential role in the lives of the American people. The Pilgrims and Puritans held so staunchly to their faith in Jesus Christ that they endured persecution in their native England and then left for the New World where they would be free to worship God as they chose.

At the cost of many lives and much hardship, these early settlers established a foothold on the North American continent with a firm reliance on God as their protector and provider. The faith of these people continued to be an important matter with them, and such matters as sin and righteousness were regarded seriously.

As the years passed, these colonizers did have periods where they neglected their faith. But in droughts, insect plagues and Indian uprisings they saw the chastening hand of God and returned to their reliance upon God with prayer and fasting. During one particularly devastating Indian war, the members of the colony turned to prayer and fasting with such vigor that it became the order of the day.

The young nation's faith in Jesus Christ was again fanned by the preaching of George Whitefield who delivered an *estimated 18,000 sermons between 1736 and 1770.*[1] Sometimes entire towns with surrounding smaller villages heard his sermons and thousands were converted.

Although not a religious man, Benjamin Franklin recorded his observations of the revival God brought about through Whitefield's preaching: "From being thoughtless or indifferent about religion, it seemed as if all the world were growing religious, so that one could not walk through the town in an evening without hearing psalms sung in different families of every street."[2]

Although this could hardly be said of present-day America, there is wide-spread interest in Christianity today. Gallup polls in 1976 and 1978 estimated that the national total of people 18 and over who claim to have had "born again" experiences numbered between 30 and 55 million. A subsequent poll placed the number at 84 million Americans (53.4% of the adult population) claiming to be born again.[3]

A significant number of the people interviewed (more than 29 million) consider themselves to be Pentecostal or charismatic Christians.[4]

Although there is great interest in religion and even Christianity today, religion in America is being undermined by several forces: cults, mysticism, humanism, liberalism and evangelical/fundamental pietism.

A 1979 issue of *Psychology Today* reports some 1,000-3,000 cults in the United States with total cult membership in this country around three million people. This includes groups such as Hare Krishna, with a membership of some 10,000; Unification Church and its 7,000 full-time members and 37,000 members overall; and Scientology, which cult experts Jim Siegelman and Flo Conway say numbers 25,000 in the U.S.

Although many of these cults vary widely in their doctrine, often their methods of indoctrination and holding their recruits are remarkably similar.

Psychiatrist John Clark testified in court about the conversion process of Sun Moon's Unification Church. He said that it included isolation, sleep deprivation, a protein-deficient diet, lengthy lecture, peer pressure and something they call "love-bombing" — showering new recruits with praise, friendship and affection.[5]

Siegelman and Conway say that a major tool of cult groups is deprivation. By depriving seekers of rest or proper nutrition or sensory input, they create an inability to think clearly, to feel or make choices. This, they say, is the beginning of mind control. Cult leaders then urge the seekers to "let go" — to release the mind, suspend doubt, stop questioning.[6]

Larry Spencer, who defected from Hare Krishna in San Diego, told *Time* how he was programmed. "They wake you up at 4 a.m. and you start chanting over and over. You're not really there, you're so tired. They pile on the spiritual answers, but you don't have enough time to think about whether they make sense. Every activity you do is what they tell you to do..."[7]

In addition to similar methods, the cults frequently appeal to people in similar situations. "To those who feel disoriented by the modern world, cults promise certainty in place of alienation, purpose in place of aimlessness. Cults also offer a substitute family where a reluctant adolescent or post-adolescent can put aside the anxieties of adulthood."

Siegelman and Conway say that the most susceptible to the cults are young people—middle or upper class. They say that this group is the "most imaginative" and are "people actively searching for answers or purpose."

After interviewing 100 people involved in cults, Margaret Singer observed that "many participants joined these religious cults during periods of depression and confusion, when they had a sense that life was meaningless. Cults supply ready-made friendships and ready-made decisions about career, dating, sex and marriage, and they outline a clear 'meaning of life.'"[8]

In addition to those groups which are readily recognized as cults by the general public, other cults are establishing themselves as more acceptable in society somewhat like the Mormons, Jehovah's Witnesses and Christian Science have done in the past. I would consider the six million Americans involved in TM and 170,000 in EST in this category.[9]

What must be done to counter this tremendous growth of the cults?

Christianity Today points out some excellent guidelines in dealing with the cults in their June 29, 1979 article entitled "Countering the Cultic Curse":

1) *Jesus' Principle.* Examine our leaders and discern when self-interest or false teaching begins to erode their ideals.

2) *The Principle of Acts.* Men and women must be hungry for spiritual truth, but not so naive that they will accept anything they are told. We must discover people's needs and meet them so that they need not turn to some false teacher to supply what the church ought to supply.

3) *Paul's approach.* Church discipline should fit the offense and should be done with gentleness. "If cult leaders had been dealt

with properly before they became aberrant, many movements may not have started." Churches must be informed about the cults so they can counteract them from the start.

Many Americans also are involved in mysticism. One evidence of this interest in mysticism is that some two million citizens consult astrologers, while millions more purchase books and consult the approximately 1,200 newspapers that carry daily astrological columns.

A Gallup organization youth survey revealed that 40% of American teenagers believe in astrology. That figure represents about 10 million teenagers, particularly young girls, who believe that the characteristics and shifting positions of the stars influence the daily events of their lives.[10]

Approximately four million practicing witches are registered with witchcraft centers in the United States. Sybil Leek, a self-styled British witch as well as a medium, says the witch population has increased 40% in the past five years.[11]

Arthur Lyons writes in his book *The Second Coming: Satanism in America:* "Satanism is not only present in Europe, but in the United States as well. In fact, the United States probably harbors the fastest-growing and most highly organized body of Satanists in the world."

Hal Lindsey, the author of *Satan is Alive and Well* on *Planet Earth*, reports an interview he had with Commander Bob Vernon of the Los Angeles Police Department. This interview revealed some signs of the occult explosion.

"Do you see indications of witchcraft or Satanic cults in the Los Angeles area?"

"Yes, and they're increasing all the time. We've found evidence of animals, mostly dogs, who have been skinned and all the blood drained from them. We discovered through talking with some of the cult members that the blood is put into caldrons, mixed with LSD, and then used as a drink during rites or ceremonies."

"Where are some of these cults located?"

"Many live in communes. Our Metro squad made a raid in a canyon where they had to let down ropes to get into the area and haul up the occupants. They were living in the most primitive way you can imagine—just a short distance from one of the most affluent neighborhoods in the country — indulging in acts of sexual deviation, pagan ceremonies, and rites which defy imagination."

"You've talked about animal blood sacrifices. Have you ever found evidence of human sacrifices?"

"A highway patrolman apprehended a man who was said to have killed another man and eaten his heart. When the officer searched him, he found knuckles of a human in the suspect's pocket. He was part of a Satanic cult."

"Do you have an explanation for the trend toward witchcraft, Satanism, and some of these other bizarre cults?"

"For one thing, I know there is a spiritual hunger among people today. Many of them have gone to a church and haven't found the answer to that hunger. Someone comes along and offers them a feeling of belonging, a sense of being loved by a group and they fall for it."[12]

At the other end of the spectrum from the "experience-oriented" followings are those who put their faith in the religion of humanism, which is man's efforts to solve his problems apart from God. *The Humanist Manifesto*, published in 1933, attacks Christianity. Although many people would call it a philosophy or theory, humanism is in reality a religion. *The Humanist Manifesto I* nine times calls its beliefs a religion.

This humanistic trend in America's religious experience has surfaced strongly in the movement of liberalism in today's churches. Since the 1800's, an incredible flood of liberalism has infiltrated the American Christian community. Liberalism occurs when people no longer hold to the Word of God as their final authority. Ignoring the Word of God as the foundation for their faith, the liberals build on the soft clay of human wisdom with disastrous conclusions. Pastors and theologians who subscribe to liberalism have led many people astray.

One individual attended a liberal church for 34 years before finding Christ as her Savior outside the church. "I wish somebody would have presented the gospel to me sooner because I had been searching for truth since I was 6," she said. "I'm four years old in my Christian life now, and I'm still throwing off some of those old ideas. I still have trouble sometimes in thinking of God as personal rather than in the nebulous way that I was brought up to believe in."

In the book *Death of a Nation*, John Stormer lays out some of the issues being grappled with in the liberal church.

> The church and churchmen are divided over whether or not God's laws against premarital sex still apply...they are divided over whether or not there are any absolutes of right and wrong...and the church is divided, surprisingly enough, over whether or not God still exists!

Robert Altizer, who began the God is Dead movement, speaks for some in the liberal movement when he says, "The God is Dead credo is still alive and well. The most important evidence that God is dead is the hopelessness in today's world. Moral judgments can't be made anymore."

Other church leaders have similar views. Dr. Joseph F. Fletcher, professor of ethics at Cambridge Episcopal Theological School, favors amending the Ten Commandments to read: "Thou shalt not covet, ordinarily. Thou shalt not kill, ordinarily. Thou shalt not commit adultery, ordinarily.

"In other words," Fletcher says, "for me there are no rules—none at all...anything and everything is right or wrong according to the situation—what is wrong in some cases is right in others...a situationist would discard all absolutes except the one absolute: always to act with loving concern."[13] This philosophy is exactly in line with humanism's teaching of situational ethics.

The World Council of Churches is an organization that hammers some of the liberal viewpoints into actions. U.S. Catholic theologian Avery Dulles feels that the W.C.C. has been progressively drawn into political and social activism that makes little reference to the theological tradition.

One example of such social activism is the W.C.C. grant to "Toward Racial Justice." This organization is accused of inciting racial hatred among blacks. Heavy on political consciousness-raising, they give a once-over-lightly to traditional belief.

One statement from a W.C.C. piece of literature was classic: "Mainland China is the only Christian country in the world."[14] That's a pretty confusing statement. Especially in view of some of the persecution of Bible-believing Christians that has taken place there in the past.

Another example of World Council of Churches activities is their plan to donate office space for an ecumenically sponsored program to promote the reunification of North and South Korea and democratic forms of government there. The purpose is to mobilize Christian support for a wider and more productive dialogue between the two Koreas.[15]

Like many of W.C.C.'s projects, this program has some very laudable objectives. In the vast majority of the projects, however, the emphasis is on depending on man's limited strength to bring about imperfect good, rather than depending on God for His infinite strength to bring about His perfect results. In this way, much of the liberal movement has similarities to humanistic thought.

A great deal of dialogue is passing back and forth in the liberal church over two controversial issues: homosexuality and the ordination of women. The homosexual issue is a particularly explosive one in this day of increasing agitation for homosexual rights.

The Rev. Troy Perry, the founder of a network of more than 100 churches geared toward homosexuals, is a self-styled gay minister. Perry said he founded the Universal Fellowship of Metropolitan Community Churches more than 10 years ago because "institutionalized religions" did not evangelize the gay community the way they were supposed to. Instead, "they locked us out as some sort of leper outcasts."

Perry reasons, "Jesus Christ came to die for all people — not just a segment. Jesus came to save me from my sins, not my sexuality."[16]

True, Jesus did come to die for all people. And He did come to save us from our sins. But I believe that the Bible clearly points out homosexuality as sin (Leviticus 20:13). God is capable of saving people from any sin and through His regenerating Spirit making them new creatures in Christ.

The issue of ordaining women in the church is another thorny one being debated in the church. Women's struggle for new status and new roles in religion was noted the top religion story of the 1970's by members of the Religion Newswriters Association.

All but six of the 62 people polled included in their list "the story of women's successful fight for ordination in the Episcopal Church in the United States, the struggle of women to achieve 'equal rights' in Roman Catholicism, the ordination of women as rabbis in Judaism's reform and Reconstructionist movements and the greatly increased number of women enrolled in theological seminaries."[17]

Without question, religion continues to play an important role in the lives of Americans today. And, according to the Gallup poll, Christianity continues to be the overwhelming choice of most Americans as their "religion." With some 50 to 84 million people over 18 claiming to be "born again," one would think that society would reflect this, the most common belief of its people.

But frequently, as you look around this nation, you see little evidence of the Christian beliefs of its people. Crime is rampant in the streets of most large cities. Families are being torn apart. Education is being reduced to baby sitting. Government is losing the respect of the governed. And religion is failing to meet people at their point of need. I believe the reason is because of the fifth problem with religion in America: evangelical/fundamental pietism. Originally pietism rejected worldly entertainments and emphasized Bible study, fellowship and the participation of laymen in the spiritual ministry of the church.

This emphasis on the devotional aspect of the Christian life has produced great blessings throughout the Christian world. But in today's society, the pendulum has swung to such an extreme that it has, in the words of David O. Moberg, "...led many selfishly to try to escape the world and live lazily in separation from it while waiting for Christ's coming instead of working in it until His return..." All too often, the Christians of the 20th century have simply withdrawn from the battle.

Dale Z. Dawson faced up to this fact in his own life and wrote somewhat of a confession for *Worldwide Challenge*.

"I am proud of where we've been as a nation, afraid of where we're headed and ashamed of the large part I have played in changing the direction of this great land.

"My guilt lies in the fact that I did nothing. I've never voted. Worse than that, I have never even bothered to register. My attitude has always been, 'Let George do it. The crooks will get into office anyhow.'

"By sitting on the sidelines for 35 years, I, like millions of others across this land, am able to take credit for many things: social decay; moral decay; an even larger gap between the generations and the races; corruption in government, business, entertainment and education.

"But my largest single accomplishment (and the one which has resulted in all of the others) is that, by 'letting George do it' I permitted God to be evicted from America. We are foolish to think that we are going to go forward as a nation without God. Each piece of legislation and each social change conceived totally of human efforts has resulted in total failure.

"I pray that there is still time to change our direction as a nation. I acknowledge that it will be done only through prayer, faith and the guidance of God. I believe that the millions like me must first of all acknowledge our guilt, pray for forgiveness and then ask God's wisdom in deciding what part He would have each of us play in putting this nation back together."[18]

This separation of ourselves from society is unbiblical. Whereas God has called us to be salt and light in our society, we have developed lifestyles that will not relate to society in any way. We live the Christian life when we are at church or with other Christians, but live a totally different life (either ungodly or spiritually aloof) while we are at work or in some social setting.

That is wrong. God is interested in our involvement in society. He wants us to be godly, moral agents of change in a culture that thirsts for direction.

Unfortunately, the plight of most Christians is summed up in the words of George Verwer, who penned an alternate version to the familiar hymn, "Onward Christian Soldiers." His version goes like this:

Backward Christian soldiers, fleeing from the fight,
With the cross of Jesus nearly out of sight;
Christ our rightful Master stands against the foe,

But forward into battle we are loathe to go.

Like a mighty tortoise moves the Church of God;
Brothers, we are treading where we've often trod,
We are much divided, many bodies we,
Having different doctrines, not much charity.

Crowns and thrones may perish, kingdoms rise and wane,
But the Church of Jesus hidden does remain;
Gates of hell should never 'gainst that Church prevail,
We have Christ's own promise, but think that it will fail.

Sit here, then, ye people, join our useless throngs;
Blend with ours your voices in a feeble song.
Blessings, ease and comfort, ask from Christ the King,
With our modern thinking, we won't do a thing.

Action Points

1. Does your life contribute to the religious breakdown in society?
2. What can you do to help solve this problem?
3. What could your church do to be involved in the solution of this problem?

CHAPTER EIGHT

Solution Steps for the Church

"Upon this rock I will build My church; and the gates of Hades shall not overpower it" (Matthew 16:18).

When you hear this verse, what comes to your mind? If you're like most people, you probably envision the Church running around with the gates of hell chasing after it. The verse actually means that Christ is building His Church and it is an awesome force. It cannot be held back, even by the gates of hell. Hell is not chasing the Church, but the Church is storming hell.

Christ has always intended that the Church be a force and not a fortress. We're a marching army, not a group of people who are separated from the mainstream of what is going on in the world.

The Church in America today is unhealthy. More than half the people in this nation claim a born-again experience, and yet we find little evidence of that "salt" permeating our society. Many Christians are not living distinctive, biblical lifestyles today. It has come to the point that often you can't tell a Christian from a non-Christian.

I draw these conclusions from my current travels around the country and from a trip my wife and I took with another couple while we were in seminary. We spent seven months in a 20-foot motor home, visiting 175 of the outstanding churches in America and covering some 20,000 miles in 37 states. The churches were all evangelical and all Protestant, but represented practically ever denomination conceivable.

It was during this trip, I concluded that the church in America is unhealthy. We did see some very large churches — ones that were thriving in terms of numbers. But there was a lack of the sense of the presence of God and the power of God working supernaturally through these churches.

As I continue to travel, I run into all kinds of people who claim to be Christians, yet they have no joy, no fulfillment, no sense of meaning in their lives. I think it is rather obvious that the church is not doing its job of equipping believers.

That fact is also reflected in the thousands of surveys taken over the years by Campus Crusade for Christ staff members. These surveys reveal that some 95% of the Christians interviewed were relying on their own strength to live the Christian life. They were either ignorant of the Holy Spirit's power or uninformed as to how to tap His limitless resources. They were living what I call carnal lives.

A.W. Tozer had some interesting insights into the dryness and impotence of so many people's Christian lives:

"A generation of Christians reared among push buttons and automatic machines is impatient of slower and less direct methods to our relations with God. We read our chapter, have our short devotions and rush away, hoping to make up for our deep inward bankruptcy by attending another gospel meeting or listening to another thrilling story told by a religious adventurer lately returned from afar."

Tozer contrasts this with the commitment of others:

"Pick at random a score of great saints whose lives and testimonies are · widely known. Let them be Bible characters or well-known Christians of post-biblical times. I venture to suggest that the one vital quality which they had in common was spiritual receptivity. Something in them was open to heaven, something which urged them Godward.

"They had spiritual awareness and they went on to cultivate it until it became the biggest thing in their lives. They differed from the average person in that when they felt the inward longing they *did something* about it. They acquired the lifelong habit of spiritual response."[2]

We need to see more people in the church today with this habit of immediate response to God's leading. I long to see the church as a whole being more responsive to God. But this will happen only as there is a reawakening of the Body of Christ. Three areas need to be transformed in order for this reawakening to take place: the church's general health, the church's general awareness and the church's general involvement.

The church needs to become healthy. A healthy church is one that is demonstrating the qualities of faith, hope and love. When a church is *not* demonstrating these qualities, it is not healthy. These qualities are discussed in 1 Thessalonians turned to God from idols. A church that is of you, making mention of you in our prayers; constantly bearing in mind your work of *faith* and labor of *love* and steadfastness of *hope* in our Lord Jesus Christ." Faith, hope and love are indicators of the health of a church.

Let's take a look at each of those words. First, Paul spoke of the Thessalonians' work of faith. That implies working faith. True faith always results in actions. A truly healthy church will be demonstrating decisive acts of faith.

That can be illustrated by the fact that the Thessalonians turned to God from idols. A church that is strong in faith is believing God for supernatural things. And in response to that faith, God is doing great things among them.

A second quality that Paul speaks of is hope — a vibrant expectancy. Frankly, I believe this element is what is missing most in America. That quality hope involves having God's perspective on life. If we don't have this perspective, we begin to dry up and lose our vibrancy.

Having His perspective simply means we do not quit; we continue on. And the reason we endure is because of hope: the realization that the Lord is going to come again and He's going to make everything right. If we really believe the Lord is going to come again, we will be purifying our lives.

This principle is illustrated in 1 John 3:3: "And everyone who has this hope fixed on Him purifies himself, just as He is pure." People who know the Lord is coming, and know they will be held accountable at His coming, live with an incredible sense of intensity and purity. This was typified to me when I was a youth pastor some years ago.

Some of the parents had problems with their children keeping their rooms clean. So I told the students I was going to come by their homes during the week, take a picture of their rooms and put it on the bulletin board with their names underneath the picture. That next week I got all sorts of phone calls from parents; they could not believe what had happened. Their children's rooms were immaculate. They asked me what I did. I simply said, "Having the hope of 'Jenson's coming' within them, they purified their lives."

The point is: when we know people are coming to our homes, we clean things up. When we know Jesus Christ is coming to evaluate us for what we've done and reward us accordingly, we fix our mind on that completely, and we live with a new sense of purity.

A third quality that is spoken of is love, which refers to relational involvement. When Paul speaks in this passage, he says "labor of love." He is saying that love will involve some toil, some labor. He indicates it takes great effort and continued strain to love.

He's not talking about loving because others love me and it's joyous, but he's talking about being committed to love others no matter what. He's talking about reaching out to people and caring for people because we are concerned for them and we want to be used of God to maximize those people.

This would not be possible apart from the Holy Spirit's empowerment. Because of the love these people had, the Word of God sounded forth brilliantly from the Thessalonians to others.

In his insightful little book, *The Mark of the Christian*, Francis Schaeffer points out the importance and the imperative of love in the Body of Christ:

> As the Samaritan loved the wounded man, we as Christians are called upon to love all men as neighbors, loving them as ourselves. Second, we are to love all true Christian brothers in a way that the world may observe. This means showing love to our brothers in the midst of our differences — great or small — loving our brothers when it costs us something, loving them in a way the world can see. In short, we are to practice and exhibit the holiness of God and the love of God.

A lack of love is what has caused many churches to wither. On the other hand, the warmth of love has drawn many people to church fellowships. In their book, *The Power of a Loving Church*, Margaret and Bartlett Hess tell of the Slidells (not their real name).

When Stan and Anita met, each was rebelling against his background. Anita grew up in a strict Protestant group. Her church taught that most other people were going to hell — especially Roman Catholics.

Stan was brought up Roman Catholic. He'd been taught that all Protestants were going to hell. These two rebels decided to marry. They agreed to marry in the Catholic church and then choose later which church to attend.

Whenever the couple visited Anita's church, someone insensitively would tackle Stan about "getting saved." After attending his church, Anita decided she could never become a Roman Catholic.

The Slidells then moved to a new community and visited 10 churches. Although the buildings were beautiful, most of them were practically empty.

They visited one small church and were in turn visited by several of the members. They wanted the Slidells to join, they explained, because they desperately needed new members. People kept visiting them, but the Slidells felt the church was not concerned about them as individuals but only wanted to add to their pitifully small congregation.

At another church, they knew they were outsiders. They could not share in communion or any church benefits unless they became members.

On other visits, they found nice ministers, bored people and uncaring congregations.

Then the Slidells visited a church that seemed different — saturated with love. It was full of people who seemed excited about their Christianity. Church members greeted the newcomers, helped them find their way around and genuinely seemed to care about them.

Prepared by this atmosphere of love in the church, the Slidells warmly received the pastor for a visit in their home. He explained to them the church's concern to help meet their needs. He explained why he preached and taught the Bible and the importance of knowing Jesus Christ.

"Can't you leave us some literature to read?" Anita asked.

"Thank you for listening to us," Stan said.

"Would you like me to pray?" the pastor asked.

They responded with one voice, "Please do."

When the pastor finished praying, Stan thanked him four times for coming. Both assured him they would be in church on Sunday. Their children were learning, they said. They too were learning, and they felt loved.

Not only does the church need to be healthy, but *it also needs to be aware and involved.* Many Christians are at one of two extremes: either they have totally *withdrawn* from the battle over moral issues, or they have become totally *involved* with moral issues.

Too often, people have divided their lives into two compartments—the spiritual compartment on one side, the secular compartment on the other. This should not be happening. When Jesus Christ becomes Lord of our lives, He is to be Lord of every aspect of it, not just the "spiritual compartment."

Although it is vitally important to speak out on moral issues, our predominant concern needs to be evangelism. God has called us to see the hearts of men and women changed; then society will be changed. So, our commitment to Jesus Christ will lead us to become involved in winning people to Him, and it will also lead us to involve ourselves in some of the moral issues of our day.

Let me explain specifically why I believe we should be involved in these moral issues. First, we need to be involved because we have an authentic love for people. If I am living a righteous life under the control of the Holy Spirit, I will naturally love other people. I will be concerned and speak out against moral wrong because I'm concerned for people. I hate unrighteousness, but I love the unrighteous. These are people with problems who need to know the problem solver—Jesus Christ.

Recently I had a chance to practice this principle when I was on a plane flight. An attractive woman began flirting with me. I could have done any one of three things. I could have said, "Hey, I ought to get to know this girl." Second, I could have said, "Who does she think she is—that unholy, unrighteous, perverted..." Or I could have said the fact she has immoral inclinations is a pretty good indication there's a void in her life.

Feeling that her greatest need was to know Christ, I knew I should go back and share Christ with her. After I had explained the gospel to her through the use of the Four Spiritual Laws booklet, she said, "This is amazing. I talked with my priest for four hours this weekend about how I could know God better, and he couldn't help me. I talked to my girl friend this morning, and she couldn't help me." The upshot of it was that she prayed to receive Christ because she had a void in her life.

The second reason for being involved in moral issues is that it is a strategic way to have contact and possible evangelistic encounters with non-Christians.

You're involved either with moral people who are good people but who do not know Christ personally, or you're involved with incredibly immoral people who are a part of the problem with which you're dealing. Both of these individuals' greatest need is to know Christ personally and be transformed internally. We can tell people it's wrong to be enmeshed in pornography, but if they don't have the power to be released from that evil, they won't be able to change.

We also need to be involved in penetrating major areas of influence. We need to be developing strategies to reach media people, political figures and educators. For instance, one individual in Kansas City, Missouri, is reaching out to people in the media in that city. He prays for them, meets with them, seeks to lead them to Christ and then build them up in their faith. Once people in these areas of influence come to Christ, they need to be discipled and absorbed into the warm, loving fellowship of the church.

Why have we come to the place where the church often is not involved in these kinds of areas? Part of the reason lies in our leadership. The church needs to develop a new kind of leader. Earlier, I mentioned Alexis de Tocqueville who came to America and concluded: "Not until I went into the churches of America, and heard her pulpits aflame with righteousness, did I understand the secrets of her genius and power."

When England was in trouble, it was people like John Wesley and George Whitefield who helped turn it around. We need more great leaders. And at this time of need for great leaders, there seems to be a leadership vacuum.

Time magazine asked a variety of historians, writers, businessmen and others in public life, "What living American leaders have been most effective in changing things for the better?" The response they received demonstrated the leadership vacuum today in American government.

James Gavin, retired Army general and executive said, "I just can't find any outstanding leaders."

Douglas Fraser, United Auto Worker president, said: "I can't think of any leaders. Isn't this sad? That's what's wrong with this country!" William Buckley, conservative columnist and editor, said, "There's no one that I know of who has the potential grip on the imagination of the American people that would be conclusive enough to cause everybody to say, 'There is a leader.' "[3]

The book *Management of Organizational Behavior* points out the crucial nature of leadership.

> The successful organization has one major attribute that sets it apart from unsuccessful organizations: dynamic and effective leadership. Peter F. Drucker points out that managers (business leaders) are the basic and scarcest resource of any business enterprise.

> Statistics from recent years make this point more evident: Of every 100 new business establishments started, approximately 50 go out of business within two years. By the end of five years, only one-third of the original 100 will still be in business. Most of the failures can be attributed to ineffective leadership.

> On all sides there is a continual search for persons who have the necessary ability to enable them to lead effectively. This shortage of effective leadership is not confined to business but is evident in the lack of able administrators in government, education, foundations, churches and every other form of organization.... What we are agonizing over is a scarcity of people who are willing to assume significant leadership roles in our society and can get the job done effectively.

For several years I've been helping to produce leaders, but in 1978 I became involved in a process that greatly multiplied my effort in helping to develop people who could fill the leadership vacuum in our nation. It was at that time I accepted an invitation to become president of the International Christian Graduate University's School of Theology.

This invitation came at a time when I was helping to pastor a church in Philadelphia. We had seen some great successes there. In a period of four and one-half years the church had grown from an average of 250 in Sunday attendance to 1,300. I also had the chance to help conduct weekly training sessions for up to 75 pastors representing 22 denominations.

We saw God mightily use that time to cause some of those churches to double and even quadruple, in some cases within a year. In many cases, pastors' lives were transformed, marriages were revitalized and the churches became warm, loving, healthy bodies which God used in powerful ways.

At that time I was very fulfilled, happy and challenged with the ministry God had given me. My wife and I were committed to the people we were ministering to and felt we were having an impact on some key influencers.

That's when I got a call from Dr. Bill Bright, the president of Campus Crusade for Christ, asking me to become President of the school. I was well aware of the innovative, one-year-old school because I had done some consulting with the leader.

I knew that the school was attempting to develop a revolutionary approach to theological education, an approach that would develop not only biblical thinkers but also men and women whose hearts burned for God and who were skilled in ministry capabilities.

As I evaluated all that I had been doing and how God could maximize my life for eternity, God convinced me there was nothing more strategic than the development of leadership. He also convinced me there was a tremendous need for a new type of spiritual leadership development program. I saw the best chance for this type of school being the International School of Theology. Therefore, my wife and I joyfully accepted Dr. Bright's invitation.

The period of time since that decision has been the greatest of my life. We saw the school grow from 10 to 60 to 120 in the first three years of its existence, one of the fastest growth rates in any seminary. And we saw our first graduating class honored in June, 1981, with 18 graduates awarded master's degrees and four wives recognized for completion of the wives' development program.

One of the many exciting concepts I've seen implemented through the school is the wholesome balance between academic training and practical application. In this way, our instruction borrows from discipleship processes. If one studies the training principles of Jesus, the apostle Paul and other great leaders throughout history, a four-fold discipleship process emerges.

Simply put, these great educators did not confine themselves to the classroom, communicating just content. They made sure there was an integrated training which involved four areas: instruction, demonstration, exposure and assessment. Taking the first letters of each of these four words forms the acrostic IDEA.

I—*Instruction:* Give practical life-related instruction in evangelism, discipleship and other biblical principles.

D—*Demonstration:* A godly lifestyle needs to be demonstrated and modeled for the developing leader.

E—*Exposure or experience:* The developing leader actually needs to put into practice the principles he is learning.

A—*Assessment:* The leader then needs to have his progress assessed. Once evaluation has been made, new courses can be decided upon.

These principles are being successfully applied at the school, and the students appreciate the thoroughness this brings to their education. "I am excited about the preparation I am getting to equip me for missions and a pastoral ministry," said Ron Lewis, one of our students. "I am also encouraged to see how the academic content taught in the classroom has such practical implications."

This emphasis on practical application of studies also impressed Chuck Harman, another of our students. "There is a real effort to make the classes practical through action-point assignments," he said. "You really know that the faculty members are concerned and care about the individual students. The interaction between the students is more of mutual encouragement rather than of individual competition."

I am excited about the opportunity to help mold godly leaders. And molding godly leaders is what the International Christian Graduate University is all about.

In addition to the School of Theology, which is already in operation, the Graduate University will have schools of communication, government, education, medicine, law, humanities, business and labor. These schools will help meet the need of our society for creative, dedicated, motivated leaders who approach their vocation from a biblical perspective.

It is an exciting process, equipping powerful Christian leaders—men and women with burning hearts for God, who are creative biblical thinkers, leaders who are able to communicate the truth to others powerfully and articulately.

These are the kinds of leaders we need if the church is going to influence the world supernaturally. And these leaders needs church members with zeal and a passion to please God. If this happens, we will begin to see our churches become healthy and involved in moral issues.

Bishop Ryle eloquently sketches for us the person committed to pleasing God:

> A zealous man in religion is pre-eminently *a man of one thing.* He only sees one thing, he cares for one thing, he lives for one thing, he is swallowed up in one thing; and that one thing is to please God. Whether he lives, or whether he dies, or whether he has health, or whether he is thought foolish, whether he gets blame, or whether he gets shame, for all this the zealous man cares nothing at all. He burns for one thing; and that one thing is to please God, and to advance God's glory.[4]

Oh, that God would give us more men and women who care for just that one thing! Our churches would be different places. And our nation would be different because of it.

1. Fill in this chart, rating each group (1 - 5, with 5 being high) in Faith, Hope, and Love.
2. Determine how your church can become more aware of moral issues of our society.
3. Determine how to get more involved as a church (and as individual Christians) with these issues.

Action Points

	YOU	FAMILY	CHURCH	CHURCH LEADERS	How can I see this quality developed in one of these groups?
FAITH (Believing God for the miraculous)					
HOPE (Expectancy of the Lord's return)					
LOVE (Relational caring)					

RECOMMENDED READING

Measure of a Church, Dr. Gene Getz, Regal Books
The Mark of the Christian, Francis Schaeffer, Inter-Varsity Press
Dynamics of Church Growth, Ron Jenson and Jim Stevens, Baker
Pursuit of God, A.W. Tozer, Christian Publications
Power Through Prayer, W.M. Bounds, Baker Books

CHAPTER NINE

Education

- Dade County, Florida—A Westview Junior High student died after a classmate smashed his face with a padlock during a lunchtime brawl.
- Brooklyn, New York—A 17-year-old student at John Jay High School was shot to death in the school yard following a fight on his first day back to school. A group of students and neighborhood youths chased the gunman before he escaped.
- Los Angeles, Calif.—Gang members stabbed one victim and beat a second with a heavy belt buckle.

Many schools are becoming dangerous places, and teachers are becoming as endangered as students. One math teacher confronted a 14-year-old student who had just insulted a cafeteria worker. The girl threw her tray of hot soup and mashed potatoes in the teacher's face and began to punch her.[1]

In another incident, an intruder forced a California second-grade teacher to undress, at gunpoint, then sexually assaulted her while the class watched. The assailant took the woman's clothes and purse when he left. The children covered her with their sweaters and jackets.

A group of high school girls, who were angry over the low grades they had been given, tossed lighted matches at their teacher, setting her hair on fire. The teacher later suffered an emotional collapse.

These incidents are hardly isolated ones. The National Institute of Education estimates that 5,200 junior and senior high school teachers are physically attacked every month and 6,000 are robbed. Under these conditions, it is small wonder that psychologists say many teachers suffer from "combat fatigue," with anxiety and neuroses similar to those of soldiers coming out of war zones.[2]

Violence continues to make headlines. But violence is just one of several signs that America's public schools are in crisis. Test scores keep dropping. Debate rages over whether or not one-fifth or more adult Americans are functionally illiterate. A government-funded nationwide survey group, the National Assessment of Educational Progress, reports that in science, writing, social studies and mathematics, the achievement of 17-year-olds has dropped regularly over the past decade. Experts confirm that students today get at least 25 percent more A's and B's than they did 15 years ago, but know less.

New nationwide data indicates that mathematics skills declined in the past five years among students age 9, 13 and 17, according to NAEP. Most can handle the mechanics of addition, subtraction and other computations, but many are stumped in applying these skills to everyday problems. For example, only 42 percent of 17-year-olds could figure the area of a square when given the length of one side.

Federal programs of the 1960's aimed at wiping out illiteracy have failed, asserts a Ford Foundation study. It concludes that as many as 64 million Americans may lack the reading and writing abilities needed for today's technologies.

In nine states, more than half the adults have not completed high school. Only four percent of high school graduates have studied a foreign langauge for as long as two years. Lack of language skills have "grave implication" for the nation's competency in world affairs, according to a presidential commission report.

Rounding up the usual suspects in the learning crisis is easy enough: the decline of the family that once instilled respect for authority and learning; the influence of television on student attention span; the disruption of schools created by busing, and the conflicting demands upon the public school system, which is now expected not only to teach but also to make up for past and present racial and economic injustice. Incompetence in the teaching ranks is also being mentioned.

Another common reason for problems in education is the rise of humanism in the public schools. John Dewey, the leader of the progressive movement in education, was influential in getting humanism on a firm footing in American schools. Dewey was an atheist and a board member of the American Humanist Association. His experimental and pragmatic theories of education were under-girded by his claim that truth is relative, that absolutes are not admissible, that the evolutionary theory is valid.

Dewey rejected the traditional approach to education and proposed the following:

—Free expression of oneself (this easily becomes self-addiction and rebellion—the "I demand to do my own thing" syndrome);

—Learning through experience (this can lead one to trust his limited observations, rather than be instructed and tempered by history, teachers and Scripture);

—Making the most of the opportunities of present life (as opposed to preparation for a more-or-less remote future).[3]

Dewey and his followers succeeded in stripping from American education its final vestiges of Christian message and purpose. Since Dewey's time, the philosophical control of the schools has passed from local communities to the federal government. With the advent of federal aid to education, schools have increasingly accepted federally approved policies that feature humanistic ideals.

The results of the humanizing of the public school system have been lowered achievement (with some high school graduates unable to read), increased difficulty for teachers to teach because of discipline problems and the mushrooming incidents of classroom violence.

In addition, there is the growing problem of teachers' inability to teach. Many teachers (estimates range up to 20 percent) simply have not mastered the basic skills of reading, writing and arithmetic which they are supposed to teach. A Gallup poll also has found that teacher laziness and lack of interest are the most frequent accusations of half the nation's parents, who complain that students have less schoolwork now than 20 years ago.[4]

A number of reasons for teaching incompetence are being debated. One reason discussed has to do with the lax standards in many of the education programs at the 1,150 colleges around the country that train teachers. It also reflects on colleges generally, since teachers take more than half their courses in traditional departments like English, history and mathematics.

Research confirms the long-standing charge that one of the easiest college majors is education. W. Timothy Weaver, an associate professor of education at Boston University, found that high school seniors who planned to major in education dropped well below the average for all college-bound seniors — 34 points below average in verbal scores on the 1976 Scholastic Aptitude Test, 43 points below average in math. Teaching majors score lower in English than majors in almost every other field.[5]

Teachers Can't Teach!

Another reason for teaching incompetence, according to teachers themselves, is that they are not allowed to teach. "The teacher today is expected to be mother, father, priest or rabbi, peacekeeper, police officer, playground monitor and lunchroom patrol," says David Imig, executive director of the American Association of Colleges for Teacher Education.

Society does not support teachers, though it expects them to compensate in the classroom for racial prejudice, economic inequality and parental indifference. The steady increase in the number of working mothers (35% work full time now) has sharply reduced family supervision of children and has thrown many personal problems into the teacher's lap, while weakening support for the teacher's efforts. Says one teacher, "I know more about some of my kids than their mothers or fathers do."[6]

Students' Attitudes

Teachers also blame the problem on students them-selves. The majority of teachers agree that many students are defiantly uninterested in schoolwork. A New York panel investigated declining test scores and found that homework assignments had been cut nearly in half during the years from 1968 to 1977. Why? Often simply because students refuse to do them.

Without question, the teaching profession does have its trials. *Time* magazine gives us a glimpse of some of those trials:

"Diana, 38, has taught high school history for ten years in a mostly black Washington, D.C. school. Says she: 'I'm not really burned out, but there are a lot of problems and not much hope.'

"Homework? 'Mostly there's no homework because they can't read. Ten years ago it was different. But these kids today are the product of the time when people thought forcing blacks to learn English was unfair. Just let them speak black English and 'kinda let them do their thing' was the way it went. So they can't read. Parents are awfully upset. But when I call them to suggest they enroll their kids in remedial work, a lot of them are not interested. They just don't want to face the problem.'

"Diana finds that just maintaining order among the nonlearners keeps her from working with the 5 percent of the class...who can read well and want to learn: 'they just sit around and die of boredom while I try to keep the other kids from fighting.'"[7]

Another problem education faces is that at least two million students nationwide—a rising number of them at the elementary level—regularly cut school without an excuse. These "ghosts," as school officials call chronic truants, will hang out on streets, ride buses aimlessly and perhaps do shop-lifting. Many youngsters will skip school every second or third day, and some eventually stop going altogether. Many more children are unenrolled and uncountable.

School systems face enormous problems in fighting the truancy problem. Severe budget cuts have forced many cities to drop attendance officers. New York and Boston, for example, have cut their attendance staffs in half during the past 10 years. And teacher and parent apathy only compounds the problem. Some teachers even quietly hope that troublemakers will stay away from their classes.

"Teachers have enough worries about kids in class who can't read," says Audrey Row, assistant to Washington Mayor Marion Barry. And many parents don't care if their children skip school. Even if they do, says Concha Johnson, an anti-truancy specialist in Washington, "the parents can't control them. The kids have lost their fear of authority and nothing fazes them."[8]

Some cities, however, have made progress in combating the problem. Dallas divides the city into 22 districts, each with a youth center and special policemen. Truants are taken to the center closest to their homes.

"Then we call in the parents," says director Bennie Kelley. "We try to get to the root of the problem and get the student back to school."

Most educators believe that anti-truancy efforts should concentrate on elementary school students, solving problems before a child's truancy patterns solidify and academic performance deteriorates seriously.

Says John Kotsakis of the Chicago Teachers Union, "Schools are now being asked to be more tolerant of disruptive or criminal behavior than society."

In Washington, D.C., for example, a jealous high school boy tried to shoot his girlfriend in class. The boy was suspended briefly from school. No other action was taken. Says a teacher from that school: "If you order a student to the principal's office, he won't go. Hall monitors have to be called to drag him away."[9]

Government Hassles

With all these problems stifling education, government agencies loom over local school authorities. The size of classes, procedures, the textbooks and time allotted to study are all affected by government demands, including desegregation of classes, integration of faculty, even federal food programs.

School officials complain that teachers are bureaucratically hammered at by public health officials (about vaccination, cavities, etc.); by insurance companies (about driver education and broken windows); social workers, juvenile police, civil liberties lawyers, even Justice Department lawyers.

And in higher education, there are some 439 federal agencies with jurisdiction over some part of university life. In 1978, 26% of Harvard's total budget (or $79 million) came from the federal government, as well as 50% of M.I.T.'s ($125 million) and 46% of Princeton's ($66 million).

Colleges and universities cannot survive without government money, but whoever pays the piper often gets to call the tune. It is obvious that, despite good intentions, government influence in academia has grown, along with the red tape necessary to comply with rules.

One example of this growing problem is the case of Pennsylvania's Grove City College, a small, religiously oriented school that, on principle, has never taken a penny in federal aid. The government sent Grove City a letter calling it a "recipient" of federal aid, and requested school officials to sign a paper assuring the school's compliance with provisions of Title IX of the 1972 Education Amendments (requiring equal opportunity for women).

Grove City College did not reply. It was not a "recipient" nor had it discriminated against women. Still, the government has said it will view tuition aid funds granted to individual students at Grove City as a form of federal support, and has threatened to withdraw them unless the school sends in its forms.

Rising Costs of Education

Public school education is one of the nation's largest single government activities—bulging with 41 million pupils. Current expenditures (federal, state and local) run to $95 billion—more than double the $41 billion in 1970. It cost the educational system an estimated $2,150 per year for each student—up from $816 in 1970. So vast and costly an educational system does not cheerfully react to criticism or adapt to change.

But in order to survive, the system needs to change. Many inner-city school systems, especially, are facing huge deficits. Chicago, for example, as the nation's third largest school system, faced an operating deficit of $43 million in 1978. Controversy began to brew in the following year about school administration incompetence that led to a deficit of possibly millions more.

Like many other inner-city school systems, Chicago's has long lived with deficits caused by expensive "special education" programs, as well as soaring payroll and energy costs and time lags in getting reimbursements from state and federal governments (such government payments make up 60% of Chicago's $1.4 billion annual budget).[10]

So vast and costly is the public educational system nationwide that it does not react to criticism nor adapt to change. But in order to survive, the system needs to change.

"There is really only one great problem in American education," says Dr. Max Rafferty, former California State Superintendent of Public Instruction, in his book, *Suffer, Little Children*. All other problems stem from it—"this is the tragedy of declining standards."

He adds that there has been a major shift in educational theory, placing the empahsis not on rising above, altering and remolding one's environment, but on adjusting to it. This is the cornerstone of modern educational thinking. The only eternal verity is constant change and flux; all values are relative; all standards are variable.

"It's a roller-coaster philosophy of life, and it's taking us on a joy ride to nowhere," he says. Young people have been so educated to conform and trained to adjust that "in another generation or two they should be ready for the beehive."

This humanistic thinking permeates the educational system, and the increasing popularity of "value-clarification" courses is an example. More than 300,000 classroom teachers have attended workshops and summer institutes to learn how to teach the courses, and at least 6,000 school systems have offered values programs.

At first glance, the term "values-clarification" sounds good, but in reality the courses subtly teach that there are no absolute morals and guidelines. Each person must decide for himself what is right or wrong. Teachers of these courses insist that the "values-clarification" approach does not aim to instill any particular set of values.[11] Instead it helps children to arrive at moral choices independently.

"No adult knows all the answers, and the children's responses are never judged right or wrong," says University of Massachusetts education professor Sidney Simon, a popular leader in the values movement.[12]

The danger in this values education is that it is valueless and simplistic. Teachers should exert their own moral influence, and the students should not be led to believe that any opinion they have is always legitimate. Some people say that because America is pluralistic, it should not have a values base to its education. However, we as Christians should stand firm in our belief that God's Word is absolute and that morality is absolute. Therefore, we ought not apologize for standing up and declaring these absolutes in the academic arena.

For too long, Christians and moral people in America have been sitting back and have tried not to thrust their convictions on others. However, in the process many people who are *immoral* have thrust their convictions on us. If we possess truth, we must do all we can to insist that it be the basis for all activity in every sphere of societal influence.

The state of public education is bleak indeed. But the situation is not hopeless. Concerned Christians can make an impact in this situation.

Here's how. Recall for a moment the diagram in chapter three. The innermost circle in the diagram was the individual. As the individual is changed, he can have an effect on his family. A revitalized family can pump new life into a church. And a healthy, involved church can bring renewal to a world that is desperately seeking for answers.

I see the church making an impact in the world of education through a four-step method.

1) Develop a healthy model;
2) Evangelize people of influence;
3) Speak out against immorality;
4) Seek fundamental moral change.

We need to develop a healthy model. This is taking place right now as Christian schools are being developed to provide an alternative to public education. *U.S. News and World Report* stated in a June, 1981 article that half the school-age children in Boston, Buffalo, Providence, Memphis and New Orleans have chosen private schools.

The magazine also noted that one federal official estimates that every seven hours a new private school opens somewhere in the United States.[13] Many parents

appreciate the discipline in the classroom as an enhance-
ment to learning, and they like the idea of Christian ideals
being intertwined with every facet of learning.

One government official thought the development of
Christian schools is in the age-old American tradition of
"competition." He felt that the success of Christian schools
would stimulate the public schools to upgrade their
"product" to attract more students.

I am not saying that public schools should be abandoned. If God leads you to keep your children in public
schools, get involved! Participate in the PTA. Keep in
touch with your children's teachers. Support the school's
programs. And see what you can do to help change those
things that you find objectionable.

Public schools can be successful. Central High School
in Little Rock, Ark., is just one of many examples that
could be cited. This inner-city school (56 percent of the
1,900 students are black) consistently turns out Arkansas'
top young scholars and athletes and places them in the
nation's most selective colleges.

These kids really produce: 24 state athletic cham-
pionships since 1970; the nation's top high school
newspaper in 1978; 14 National Merit semifinalists in
1980; SAT scores 46 points higher than the national
average. No wonder 41 students from private schools trans-
ferred to Central last semester.[14]

We need to evangelize people of influence in education.
In high schools, several ministries are doing good work in
introducing students to Christ and instructing them in
their faith. These ministries include Young Life, Campus
Life, Youth for Christ and Campus Crusade's High School
Ministry.

Perhaps God would have you lend your support to a
local group like one of these in your area. You could offer
your home as a place for the students to meet, or you could
provide encouragement and support for the dedicated staff
members who are working with the students.

Another resource not to be overlooked is Christian
teachers. While even the most influential student leaves
high school in a few short years, teachers can remain for a

long time. Seek opportunities to win teachers to Christ, or aid those who are already Christians in their spiritual development. Offer them ideas in how they can have an impact for Christ on their students.

On the college level, Inter-Varsity, the Navigators, Campus Crusade for Christ and some denominational groups are influencing students for Christ. An instance of this impact is the Penn State campus, where at one time 450 students were participating in Campus Crusade small group Bible studies, making it probably the largest student group on campus. The staff and students contacted at least 12,500 people that year about the claims of Christ.

Occasionally the Christian groups and students pool their efforts for a major evangelistic event on the campus. For instance, at Western Washington State University, five Christian groups pooled their efforts to coordinate a three-night lecture series on campus for Campus Crusade's traveling speaker, Josh McDowell. Their efforts were rewarded when nearly half the student body heard McDowell speak during his visit to the campus and 960 requested information about Christ.

In addition to college students coming to Christ, college professors need to be confronted with the gospel. Professors, trustees, university presidents and leaders in the Department of Education all are in tremendous positions of influence. If reached for Christ, these men and women could exercise their leadership to help bring the Lord back to His proper position in the university system. Once again, He could be looked to as the source of wisdom and learning.

Few people realize that 104 of the first 119 colleges founded in America were conceived for the purpose of acquainting young scholars with the knowledge of God. This group of schools founded on Christian ideals includes Harvard, Yale, Columbia, Princeton and many other fine institutions of higher learning.

The results of Christian instruction at these schools produced many ministers of the gospel. In fact, during the colonial period, 70% of Harvard's graduates went into the ministry.

We need to speak out against immorality in education.
Speak out against the secular humanism that frames much
of the instruction in schools. Read your children's textbooks. Monitor them for humanistic teachings, advocating
of immoral practices and unjust accusations against our
country.

One Christian college teacher at a secular university
wrote a thoughtful article in *Christianity Today*, speaking
out about his concerns.

> The spiritual upsurge evident in collegians' private lives is not,
> however, significantly reflected in university curricula. Secular,
> humanistic philosophies continue to dominate course offerings
> and content...Rarely are students exposed in their curricula to an
> objective and comprehensive view of the biblical message that
> centers in Jesus Christ. Rarely are they acquainted with the depth
> of influence that the Christian world view has had on Western
> values.
>
> I have been appalled at the lack of biblical knowledge shown by
> senior, graduate students, and even incoming seminary students
> educated at secular universities. Abraham Lincoln would be even
> more appalled. He once said that if he had to choose between a
> college education without a knowledge of the Bible and a
> knowledge of the Bible without a college education, he would
> choose the latter.[15]

*We need to see fundamental moral changes in
education.*
Some Christian leaders feel that without change in this
vital arena, cataclysmic consequences could occur. Dr.
Charles Malik, former president of the U.N. General
Assembly, is one of these leaders:

> No civilization can endure with its mind as confused and disor-
> dered as ours is today. All our ills stem proximately from the false
> philosophies that have been let loose in the world and that are now
> being taught in the universities. Save the university and Western
> civilization is saved, and therewith the world.[16]

RECOMMENDED READING

The Christian Mind, Harry Blamires, Servant.
Must Our Schools Die? David H. Paynter, Moody Press.
Listen, America, Jerry Falwell, Doubleday-Galilee.

Action Points

1. Take a good hard look at your local schools. Are the students receiving a good education? If not, see what you can do to help change things. Consider running for the school board, or help recruit a moral, godly person to run for such a position.
2. See what can be done to bring in teachers who are not only capable at instructing, but also have good moral lives and can serve as positive examples to their students.

CHAPTER TEN

The Menacing Media

Click. The mother of a family of four flips the "on" button and the TV set glows to life. The entire family gathers for an evening of entertainment.

As the evening progresses, the family views one show where a man and woman meet at a society affair. He becomes uproariously drunk and they proceed to her apartment. By the time she can fix a cup of coffee, he has staggered into the bedroom, shed clothes and collapsed into bed. The woman, with steaming coffee pot in hand, surveys the scene, then returns the coffee pot to the stove.

Wordlessly she glides back into the bedroom. A zipper whispers and the woman's dress slips to the floor. The eye of the camera zooms in on the woman's back as the rest of her clothes fall to the floor. She slides into bed with her guest and softly runs her hands through his hair. The man awakes, embraces her and...

At the conclusion of the program, click, click, click. Another channel, another story. This time the entertainment centers around a model young man, whose life goes haywire. He ascends a tower at a university campus and methodically begins killing people with a high-powered rifle. One body after another crumples into a lifeless heap. Students scream in pain. Everyone else runs for cover. Finally, a sharpshooter zeroes in on the sniper and ends his hail of death with a bullet in the skull.

Click, click, click. Another channel, another program. But first a word from our sponsor. A catchy jingle about "designer jeans" is accompanied by scenes of a well-proportioned woman tightly clad in the sponsor's product. She's laughing. She's being pursued by a handsome man. She's having a good time. The obvious conclusion: wearing this product makes you sexy, attractive and popular.

Now it's time for a popular situation comedy. In this particular episode the main character lies and bluffs his

way out of a sticky problem with his wife that was caused
by another earlier lie. His situational ethics have ensnared
him.

The scenario I have described takes place night after
night in home after home across America. The names of
the programs, the characters and the advertisements may
differ, but the menu of violence, sex and situational ethics
remains the same.

Not *all* television programming is bad. But a large
portion of the prime-time programming is thoroughly
saturated with humanistic values. And with TV's pouring
their images into homes at an average of six hours a day,
can they help but make an impact on people's thinking?

Advertisers feel they can effectively promote cars,
toothpaste, clothes, mouthwash, detergent and a con-
stellation of other products. The advertisers feel that in 30-
to 60-second bursts on television, they can make a difference in their sponsors' sales.

If advertisers can make a difference with such short
segments, think of the impact six-plus hours of
programming per day can make!

Many of the views expressed during this time are
humanistic in nature. In keeping with the "non-theistic"
belief, God is largely ignored. Humanism's concept of no
absolutes shows up frequently in the situational ethics of
some of television's main characters. And humanism's idea
of sexual conduct being unrestricted is reflected in the
large amount of play given to sexual themes.

Harvard University's Project on Human Sexual
Development did a comprehensive study of television's
role in the sexual education of children. Their study
revealed some interesting patterns in programming:

  —70% of all allusions to intercourse occurs between
    unmarried couples or involves a prostitute;
  —much of television's erotic activity involves violence
    against women.

The television medium is also a strong promoter of
alcohol. Television characters drink 3.5 times per hour on
television, four times an hour during prime time. For every
time coffee is consumed on TV, alcohol is consumed 10
times. For every time milk is consumed, alcohol is con-

sumed 44 times. For every time water is drunk, alcohol is drunk 48 times.

Of course, the media cannot bear the full blame for the alcoholism rate in this nation. But the fact that it so constantly places alcohol before the consumer and presents it in such an alluring context (i.e. drinking is macho, drinking makes you sexually attractive, you have a good time when you drink, etc.) cannot help but influence people to drink.

This is especially true for youth in America, among whom alcoholism has reached alarming portions. A March 6, 1978 issue of *Business Week* outlines the situation: "Teenage 'problem drinkers' now number about one million—at least double the number five years ago, according to some experts."

Television Viewing Habits

Academic performance may also be affected by heavy TV viewing. While the experts continue to debate its effects, some alarming facts have been accumulated. By age 18, the average American has spent an estimated 15,000 hours in front of the set, far more time than in school.

In Bedford, Mass., psycho-physiologist Thomas Mulholland and Peter Crown, a professor of television and psychology at Hampshire College, have attached electrodes to the heads of children and adults as they watched TV. While viewing TV, the subjects' output of alpha waves increased, indicating they were in a passive state as if they were "just sitting quietly in the dark." The implication: "TV may be a training course in the art of inattention," they suggest.

Groups of several hundred three- and four-year-olds have been studied as they watch TV at home and in nursery school. The researchers, professors Jerome and Dorothy Singer, who head Yale University's Family Television Research Center, are convinced that "heavy TV viewing stunts the growth of imagination in the crucial ages between three and five. Such children make up fewer games and imaginary playmates."[1]

According to other studies, by age 15 the average American child witnesses between 11,000 and 13,000 acts of violence on TV. At the moment, the debate rages among the experts about the implications of such a barrage on a child's moral sensitivities.

In addition to the entertainment media, the news media have also reflected humanistic bias. Although the philosophy of news is supposedly the fair and impartial reporting of both sides of the issues, this has not been the case. Increasingly, advocacy journalism has come into prominence, which means that the side of the issue that the reporter favors is given the most favorable presentation, or, in some cases, the only presentation.

Frequently the stories covered in the news media, or the way they are covered, reflect a humanistic bias. One of the innumerable examples that could be cited occurred in the November 25, 1979 issue of *Parade* magazine. The lead article, entitled "Public School Book Censors Try It Again," showed some people standing around a book bonfire.

Although the title, picture and article gave the impression that some wild-eyed fanatics were obstructing freedom of the press, in reality the people featured were Mel and Norma Gabler, a humble Christian couple. This couple studies modern textbooks and points out those teachings that are un-American, contrary to traditional moral values, or twist history and make unfair presentations of the free-enterprise system. Then they send their evaluations to parent groups. Humanists call this restricting freedom. Concerned Christians call it promoting morality. *Parade* magazine took the humanistic slant.

The question of how much the humanistic ideals presented by the media affect the actions of people who view it is hard to put into statistics. The Bible says, "As a man thinketh in his heart so is he." So as people think of the amorality and sexual license presented in the media and continue to expose themselves to these ideals, their actions will be affected.

An example of violence on the screen breeding real-live violence occurred as a result of the movie "The Warriors," a film about gangs. The March 19, 1979 issue of *Time* magazine reported that three young men were killed as a result of Warrior-inspired fights and other brawls breaking out in movie houses in several cities.

A Boston gang member returning from seeing the movie even yelled, "I want you!"—a line from the movie—immediately before gang members fatally stabbed 16-year-old Marty Yakubowicz.

In spite of the violence surrounding "The Warrior" showings, the all-powerful "bottom line" prevailed. The *Time* article closed with this statement:

> "The furor over 'The Warriors' has made everyone in Hollywood a little nervous. But it cost less than $6 million, and its receipts, so far, are likely to drown any second thoughts about releasing the rest of the gang films."

Even as "The Warriors" engendered violence in its viewers, pornographic literature and films have been known to foster immoral sexual behavior. Many cases of this kind have been documented, including the case of Kenneth Earl Adams. On two separate occasions, he kidnapped at knifepoint, a 17-year-old girl and a 20-year-old girl. He then took them to a secluded place and sexually assaulted them.

Adams testified at his court trial that he had been preoccupied with pornographic literature. He said that when the adult book stores opened in his city, "I couldn't believe it (hardcore pornography) existed. I had never heard of anything like this."

He became obsessed with reading these books and magazines. "...the books became more important than my family," he said. When he was arrested, the police found 177 pornographic books in the trunk of Adams' car.

Adams further testified in court that he had abducted the girls in a search for partners to "act out" what he read and saw in his books.

Numerous other examples could be cited of the connection between obsession with pornographic materials and immoral behavior. But that doesn't stop these materials from being produced. In fact, those involved in the industry are going to new lengths to shock their audiences.

The J. Walter Thompson Co., one of the largest advertising agencies in the world, points out the reason behind this. "As each medium makes more and more intense efforts to grab our attention, the level of our resistance rises. What shocked us yesterday does not shock us today...One day's sensation is the next day's hohum."[2]

The movie "Caligula" is an example of a film that seemed to go out of its way to shock people. One New York movie chain executive commented, "It's as hard-core as anything you'll see in a porn theater...I believe even porn houses would be reluctant to book it because of the violence, the bloody mutilation."

In San Bernardino, California, when this movie was booked into a family theater for a three-week run, the Christian community campaigned for removal of the film. Concerned Christians distributed leaflets urging people to voice complaints about the film to the mayor and the police chief. They also planned a protest rally to be held outside the theater if other pressures failed to remove the movie. Largely as a result of the actions of the Christian community, the movie was closed and the theater manager was fined for showing an "adult" film without a license, in violation of a zoning ordinance.

Bill Bauman, one of the organizers of the campaign to remove the film, remarked, "This is important because it shows people that things like an obscene movie can be stopped. Christians can see results when we express our views to those in authority."

Cases like the removal of "Caligula" from a city are examples of what can happen when Christians decide to take seriously Christ's command to be "the salt of the earth." When the Body of Christ stands together on a moral issue, it can have an impact on its community.

The same four-step strategy for change that we applied to education in our last chapter can be used successfully with the media. As we develop healthy models, evangelize people of influence, speak out against immorality and work for fundamental change, I believe we will see great things happen in the media.

Let's examine each of these steps. *First, we need to develop a healthy model in the media.*

Currently, films are being produced to educate the audience and stimulate them to action. An example of this kind of film is "Assignment Life," a movie which clearly points out the true nature of abortion and its danger to our society.

Another example of this kind of film is James Dobson's film series, "Focus on the Family." This series provides insightful instruction on how homes can be brought back into line with God's principles.

Films also are being produced which portray the Christian message. Examples of this include the movie "Jesus," which was produced by Inspirational Films, and a film on the life of Paul which is being developed. Numerous other Christian films have been developed and can be rented for showings at churches, civic clubs, neighborhoods and for entire communities. You can write Gospel Films, Campus Crusade for Christ Media Distribution, Worldwide Pictures, Ken Anderson Films, Mark IV Productions and other groups for additional information (see appendix).

Christian films and television programs are essential as models. If all the trash could be taken off the television stations and out of the movie houses, we would need to be prepared with an alternative model to fill that vacuum. We must be able to relate to the non-Christian with tools that are most effective in reaching him. For instance, Christian Broadcasting Network is producing a Christian soap opera for that very purpose. We need this kind of innovative thinking in order to reach the maximum number of non-Christians.

In addition to the development of good models in television programming and films, we need more good models in radio programming and in the print media—magazines and newspapers. Currently some excellent radio programming and magazines are being produced, but we need still more and in ever-increasing quality. This is important if good moral principles and the Christian message are to be disseminated in the maximum way.

We need to evangelize people of influence in the media. We can begin by finding out who the leaders of the media are: network presidents, television producers, leaders in advertising and regulatory agencies, actors, actresses, publishers and key editors of newspapers, magazines and books, owners and managers of radio stations.

Once we have determined who the leaders are, we need to set out to reach them with the message of Christ. Many of these people are hard to meet, so a possible method to contact them is through "networking." This method entails reaching the individual through the network of people around him.

For example, you might focus on the editor of a big-city newspaper. Find out who this individual's friends are. Where do his children go to school? Once you have determined the answers to these questions, seek to win the editor's friends and family to Christ.

Through them you might have an opportunity to present the gospel message to the editor. At a later time, you might even see Christian principles beginning to emerge as a guiding force in his decisions as editor of the newspaper.

We need to speak out against immorality in the media. It is exciting to see what many groups are doing in this area. The Coalition for Better Television represents a number of conservative organizations that are speaking out against immorality and attempting to influence sponsors of television shows in an effort to eliminate some of the objectionable programming.

The Rev. Donald Wildmon is heading up this effort and seeing some outstanding successes. An ordained Methodist minister, Rev. Wildmon preached in churches for 20 years in his home state of Mississippi. Several years ago he was looking for a television show that he and his family could watch. As he flipped the channels, he could find nothing but sexual innuendo, profanity and violence on television.

Instead of just muttering about the evils of television, he decided to do something. He launched the National Federation for Decency, giving up his church ministry. Operating out of a three-room office, assisted by a staff of two, his work has shaken the television establishment.

Wildmon managed to do this by training volunteers to assist in surveying television shows and evaluating them in their content of sex, violence and undermining of morality. Armed with these results and advance notice of other undesirable programming, he organized letter-writing campaigns to the sponsors of these programs. If this doesn't prove successful, he urges boycotts of the sponsors' products. He also urges people to write positive, encouraging letters to sponsors who advertise on good programs.

The most spectacular results of the Coalition's efforts occurred in June, 1981, when Chairman Owen Butler of Procter & Gamble, TV's biggest customer ($486.3 million in commercials) announced that within the past year his company had pulled out of 50 TV movies and series episodes, including seven of the 10 series that Wildmon had cited as "top sex-oriented." Now other companies are conferring with Wildmon to see if they can avoid boycotts through mending their ways.

The exciting thing about this occurrence is that it proves we don't have to sit idly by and have programs promoting immorality continually flooding the airways. We can make a difference! We do not represent a small fraction of the population of this nation; we speak for the majority when we say we are fed up with television programming as it is and want better, more constructive, morally upright programs.

Get on the mailing lists of organizations like the National Federation of Decency (see appendix). And lend them your support by writing letters and evaluating current television programming. It is through the efforts of thousands of informed, concerned citizens across the country that we can have a say in what is broadcast on television.

We must see fundamental change in the media. The media must become more God-honoring if our society is to survive. It cannot continue to spew forth filth, immorality, violence and illicit sex into our living rooms without disastrous consequences. The media has incredible influence in our society and it must be changed.

And until it does change, we must carefully monitor our own television watching habits. Otherwise, we will see our own thinking subtly pressed into the world's mold instead of the mold set before us by the example of the Son of God.

Try going a week without television. You'll probably find its effect on you has been similar to a powerful drug. You might even sense some "withdrawal pains." But you will find that you have much more opportunity for quality time with your family and for other interests. A long-term result might be that you decide to scale down your television-viewing time in favor of other worthwhile activities.

Action Points

1. Look for humanistic influences in the media. Develop the ability to identify issues that have their roots in humanistic thought. Humanistic ideas rarely are labeled clearly. But they directly affect media programming (e.g., how sex and morality are treated) and points of view that are expressed on social, religious and political issues.[3]

2. Write tactful and carefully reasoned letters to newspapers, television networks, local television and radio stations, sponsors of programs and legislators, expressing alternative viewpoints or critiques of their positions or programming. If you find something particularly offensive, organize a letter-writing campaign among friends and fellow Christians. A majority of Americans are theists (believers in God), but they seldom make their voices heard. You can help move them to action.[4]

3. If, however, you watch a program or read an article that glorifies the Lord or presents biblical perspectives in a positive way, express your thanks. Too often the media receive only negative reactions from Christians.[5]

4. Zero in on your own television viewing time for a moment. Total the amount of time you watch television each day. Is this a healthy amount? How is what you watch on television affecting you? Take out a pad of paper one evening and write down the ways humanism is communicated through the programs you watch at night. Realize that these ideas will have some effect on you as you continue to expose yourself to them over a period of time.

RECOMMENDED READING

Media Sexploitation, Wilson B. Key, New American Library
The View From Sunset Boulevard, Ben Stein, Basic Books, Inc.
National Federation for Decency, Box 1398, Tupelo, MS 38801 (newsletter)

APPENDIX

Films:

[Contact some of these organizations for catalogues of their films and ask for the address of a nearby distributor of Christian films.]

Gospel Films Inc., 455 Muskegon, Mi 49443

Worldwide Pictures, 1201 Hennepin Ave., Minneapolis, MN 55403

Ken Anderson Films, Box 618, Winona Lake, IN 46590

Media Distribution, Campus Crusade for Christ, Arrowhead Springs, San Bernardino, CA 92414

Quadrus Communications, 610 E. State Street, Rockford, IL 61104

CHAPTER ELEVEN

Government

Three men—a doctor, an architect and a politician—went for a long walk and they began discussing whose profession was the oldest. The doctor said, "My profession is the oldest, since God created Eve out of Adam's rib and performed a surgical operation." The architect replied: "My profession is still older, since God, just like any architect, in creating the world made it out of chaos!" "Ah," joined in the politician, "but who made the chaos?"[1]

Of course, there have been many individuals in all three branches of government who have carried out their responsibilities capably and maintained their integrity. But too often some of our government leaders have led this great nation down a precarious path. Perched dangerously on a narrow ledge, America potentially faces today a long fall into the deep gorge of internal conflicts on the one side and an equally perilous drop on the other side into the forbidding waters of pressures from abroad.

Government in America is in trouble. The order of the day has been mushrooming bureaucracy, expanding corruption, mass disillusionment and loss of confidence in the institutions of power. Five major "lacks" have contributed to the plight of American government today—the lack of positive international influence, the lack of perspective, the lack of efficiency, the lack of resolve, the lack of a moral base in leadership. Some encouraging changes have taken place under the strong leadership of President Reagan, but the problems are still resident in significant aspects of our government and need to be addressed squarely.

Our lack of positive international influence has been graphically reflected in our relationship with the Soviet Union. The Soviets have always had the goal of destroying capitalistic society. They are a nation committed to

communism and to destroying the American way of life.
"We shall surround and defeat the last bastion of
capitalism," wrote V.I. Lenin. And "when the capitalists
guard is down, we will smash them," declared Georg
Demitriov.

At the end of World War II, such talk seemed an empty
boast. At that time the United States was the preeminent
power in the world. And the Soviets were struggling to
recover from crippling losses in the war. In 1962, before the
Cuban missile crisis, the Russians had made great progress
in marching toward their goal. But when U.S. President
Kennedy challenged the Soviets, the Russians backed down
because America held most of the aces. The U.S. had the
superior weaponry, and the Soviets knew it.

Things have changed. If it came to a test of military
muscle today, it is possible that it would be the U.S. that
would be backing down. Increasingly, America is being
perceived as a second-class power militarily.

To summarize, the Soviet Union has double the offensive nuclear weaponry of the United States and 47 times
the defensive weaponry.[4] This nuclear superiority makes
obsolete the long-held strategy of Mutual Assured
Destruction (MAD). According to this theory, since the
United States could wipe out the Soviet populace with
nuclear strike and the Russians could do the same, neither
side would risk an attack.

The advent of Soviet nuclear superiority and the
upgrading of their civil defense program, making it possible
for them to save all but a few million of their people and
most of their industry, totally negates the old MAD
strategy. What U.S. president could answer a Russian
threat with a nuclear strike, knowing that a Soviet
counterattack would destroy half of America's population
when the Soviet Union would lose only less than 1
million people? The end result could be this nation
surrendering to the Communists.

Without question, the Soviet Union is making progress
toward its goal of world domination. Its bold takeover of
Afghanistan and ruthless attempts to squelch Afghan
resistance have shown to the world that the Soviet Union

is still serious about bringing more territory under its
domination.

In addition to Afghanistan, dominoes continue to fall in
Southeast Asia, Africa and with increasing rapidity in Latin
America. Strongly reinforced by the Soviet Union's main
ally, Fidel Castro, country after country in Latin America is
coming under Communist rule. America has been losing
the test of weapons and men, and perhaps even more
important, it has been losing the test of wills.

In addition to the lack of positive international influence, government is demonstrating a lack of perspective. The government and the populace have lost sight
of the real purpose of government. "A whole generation of
Americans has grown up brainwashed by television and
textbooks to believe that it is the responsibility of
government to take resources from some and bestow them
upon others. This idea certainly was alien to the founding
fathers of our country."[5]

James Madison, one of those founding fathers, spoke
about the relationship of the government and the governed:

> We have staked the whole future of American civilization, not
> upon the power of government, far from it. We have staked the
> future of all of our political institutions upon the capacity of
> mankind for self-government; upon the capacity of each and all of
> us to govern ourselves, to control ourselves, to sustain ourselves
> according to the Ten Commandments of God.

> Our founding fathers intended that individuals be the master, and
> the state the servant. Thomas Jefferson said, "Man is not made for
> the State, but the State for man." It was important to the framers
> of the Constitution that the rights of all Americans be protected
> and that the authority of every branch of government be limited. It
> was important to protect the rights of individuals.[6]

Another area where the government's lack of perspective and overcontrol has come into play is the
relationship of the church and state. This is one more area
in which the state has taken away rights that were once the
property of individuals.

The First Amendment to our Constitution was designed
to protect the American people from an established
government church, a church that would be controlled by
the government and paid for by the taxpayers. Our foun-

ding fathers sought to avoid this favoritism by separating
church and state in function. This does not mean they
intended a government devoid of God or of the guidance
found in Scripture.

The courts of this nation are taking away Americans
religious freedoms in the name of "separation of church and
state." For example, two U.S. trial courts have ruled that a
group of college students who wish to discuss religion
could not meet in the context of a public state university
that religious speech must go on elsewhere since it might
"establish religion" on the campus.

In another interesting case, a Jews for Jesus group was
meeting in a West Los Angeles home. A neighbor com-
plained and a zoning hearing was held. The Department of
Building and Safety took the position that even if one non-
resident was present, it was a public meeting and they had
a right to regulate it. The complaining neighbor apparently
moved away, laying to rest that particular controversy.
However, it left an internal policy memorandum
suggesting that the city has a right to close down home
Bible studies.

Lack of Efficiency

Increasingly in today's society, government has become
bigger and bigger, taking away more rights of individuals
and assuming those rights as their own. Among the more
obvious examples of this usurping of rights is the maze of
government regulation and red tape that can snarl ex-
pansion and progress in the economy. This has resulted in a
tremendous lack of efficiency in our government.

"A quagmire of federal and state regulations now exists
that can bog down any project, no matter how worthy,"
says Alton Whitehouse, chairman of Standard Oil Company (Ohio).

In March, 1979, after spending 50 million dollars, Sohio
abandoned its 5-year-old plan to build a 1,000-mile oil
pipeline from Long Beach, California, to Midland, Texas.

Its reason: prolonged delays in winning state and local
permits no longer made the billion-dollar pipeline
economically viable. Only 250 permits had been approved,
including the 12 required by federal agencies. The rest were

held up by state and local governments.

It wasn't the first time that local red tape had canceled a major industrial project. In 1977, Dow Chemical Company aborted plans to build a $500 million petrochemical complex in the San Francisco Bay area. After two years of negotiations with county, state and federal officials, Dow had obtained only four of the 65 permits needed. It was costing the company $200,000 a month just to keep permit applications current.[7]

But it's not just big business which faces the mountain of red tape and has to pass the cost of dealing with that red tape on to the consumer. The small businessman also faces this battle, which is one that can cripple his business efforts.

The October, 1980, issue of *Reader's Digest* reports the story of George S. Lockwood. It will give you insight into what battling red tape is all about:

> Early in 1972, Lockwood discovered that the supply of abalone, a tasty Pacific snail, was declining, demand was increasing and the price per pound was rising sharply. If Lockwood could domesticate abalone he could dramatically increase its production. This would bring down its price, create jobs and, Lockwood hoped, make a profit.
>
> After perfecting a complicated technique for spawning abalone and raising the young snails to adulthood plus raising $1.25 million, Lockwood was ready to begin his operation. Or so he thought.
>
> First, he had to obtain the necessary permits from the Monterey, California, planning, building and finance departments, along with licenses from five different offices of the California Department of Fish and Game. Then the federal government entered the picture.
>
> Lockwood had to secure a permit from the Treasury Department's Bureau of Alcohol, Tobacco and Firearms in order to get a supply of undenatured alcohol to check abalone tissue for disease. He also needed chloral hydrate which he used to sedate the snails in order to induce them to spawn. The need for this drug meant another permit and lengthy inspections by the Food and Drug Administration.
>
> In August, 1975, Lockwood and his 24 employees were about to launch a complex week-long experiment that would determine if the whole process was viable. Just minutes before they were to start, two inspectors from California's Division of Industrial Safety (CAL-OSHA) arrived at the door, saying they had heard there was a

"serious ozone hazard in the abalone breathing room."

Lockwood had no "abalone breathing room"; he did have a small ozone generator, which he had purchased at the suggestion of another government agency. Reluctantly, he called off the experiment. Once past the door, the inspectors admitted that they were not equipped to measure ozone levels themselves. But while they were there, they would conduct "a thorough inspection of all other aspects of safety."

At the end of the day they cited Lockwood for 14 violations and fined him $265. Some of the complaints were legitimate. But others seemed ridiculous. An extension cord had been run across the floor. Because he was afraid someone might trip over it, Lockwood hung it over a nail on the wall. That resulted in a citation for "using a flexible supply cord as a substitute for fixed wiring of the building."

Lockwood had a first-aid kit as required by law, but he didn't have a letter from a physician saying that the kit's materials were adequate. He also had a conveyor belt to carry boxes between the first and second floors. This the inspectors, decreed, was a safety hazard. Someone could catch his finger in the belt or pulley drives. The conveyor would have to go. One month later an employee carried a heavy box upstairs and suffered a hernia.

After one particularly irritating battle with the bureaucratic maze, Lockwood told his wife, "I've been a businessman for 20 years, and I'm being treated like a criminal by my own government."

The embattled businessman appealed 10 of his citations—at considerable cost in time and effort—and succeeded in reversing seven. The CAL-OSHA inspectors brought ozone-measuring equipment to the facility—and found that ozone level was lower than it is in Los Angeles.

Lockwood faced a new set of skirmishes from county, state and federal environmental agencies. Since 1974, Monterey Abalone Farms had discharged water containing snails' organic waste into the ocean. Then Lockwood learned that he would have to obtain the same permit that was required for a large sewage treatment plant. He protested that abalone had "gone potty" unregulated by government for at least one million years. Besides, chemical tests proved that the water his firm discharged was actually cleaner than the water it took in. Wasn't that ground for exemption? The California Regional Water Quality Control Board said, "No."

Slowly, despite what seemed to be government harassment at almost every level, Lockwood's business is beginning to flourish. Orders from customers are increasing. Finally after years of effort, he will be close to showing a profit.

Even though Lockwood believes that most of his major problems are now behind him, he still spends about 60 percent of his time keeping up with government forms. But worst of all, he lives with the numbing fear that at any time, almost any government agency could come in and shut down his business.

Government inefficiency is not only reflected by the jungle of rules, regulations and red tape that plague our businesses, but also by the waste of our tax dollars on projects of dubious ends. Here's a sampling:

$3 billion stolen annually from health programs—yet the federal government has fewer people investigating the theft than it has manicuring the White House lawn.

$6.5 billion a year for the Pentagon to buy five times as many routine supplies (not weapons) as are actually used, 80% of which are later scrapped in unused condition or sold for pennies on the dollar.

$85,000 per minute to pay interest on the "National debt," costing a total of $318 billion since World War II.

$375,000 for a Pentagon study of the frisbee.[8]

Economist Milton Friedman points out that currently more than 40% of our income is disposed of on our behalf by government at the federal, state and local levels. He points out in his book *Free to Choose* that as late as 1928 federal government spending amounted to only 3% of the national income.[9]

In his book *Restoring the American Dream*, Robert Ringer sums up America's situation this way: "As taxation and regulation of business increase, motivation to produce will die, leading inevitably to a nationalization of industry. This is the step which will take America from the decaying stage to the death stage. It happened in Greece; it happened in Rome; it happened in every civilization that tried to provide the free lunch for its citizens and then blamed the businessmen for its financial collapse."

Lack of Purpose and Resolve

In addition to the government's lack of positive international influence, lack of perspective and lack of efficiency, it also suffers from a lack of purpose and resolve. These days of vacillating foreign and domestic policy and decisions, based on public opinion polls of constituents, are a far cry from days past. In the beginning of our nation, the resolve of individuals was so strong that they committed their entire lives to ideals.

This sense of resolve and purpose is reflected in the words of John Adams at the Third Continental Congress in 1776:

> Before God I believe the hour has come. My judgment approves this measure, and my whole heart is in it. All I have, and all that I am, and all that I hope in this life, I am now ready to stake upon it. And I leave off as I began, that live or die, survive or perish, I am for the Declaration. It is my living sentiment, and by the blessing of God it shall be my dying sentiment, independence now, and independence forever![10]

Fifty-six men signed the Declaration of Independence, pledging their lives, their fortune and their sacred honor to making this declaration a reality. That kind of resolve is practically unheard of today. But for these men, it was their commitment. And they all knew that this commitment might lead to their being hung as traitors if the war was not successful.

Of these 56 men who signed the declaration, 14 lost their lives as captive soldiers or casualties in the war for independence. Many lost their sons and saw their lands and properties devastated. Although most of them were men of means, they knew that liberty and freedom were more important than security.

Lack of a Moral Base in Leadership

Closely aligned with the lack of purpose and resolve in government today is the lack of morality in leadership. Nowhere has this been more evident than in the scandals that have rocked our nation's capital in the past few years. Questionable ethics abounded in the Watergate controversy. And the "Koreagate" investigation showed that the same ethics were present in Congress as well as in the Executive branch. The Abscam operation, carried out by the FBI, showed that legislators were very willing to forget their principles if the price was right.

These, and other well-publicized lapses by elected officials, have soured the American people toward government. The phrase "crooked politician" has become a cliché. As a result, many people have lost confidence in their government.

This lack of a moral base undergirding our government is a critical problem. With so many instances of lack of ethics and morality in the government, it is not surprising that in a *U.S. News & World Report* survey on American leadership, 76.1 percent of the people questioned named moral integrity as one of the most-needed attributes in today's leaders. Courage was the second most frequently named attribute, polling 55.2 percent of the votes.

Lawrence D. Cohen, mayor of St. Paul, Minn., commented on qualities needed for leadership: "If cynicism and apathy are to be reversed, the national leadership must take stands from a position of honesty and integrity."[11]

Moral integrity based on a firm reliance on God has long been established as a standard for the leadership of this country. For example, government leaders have been setting aside one day a year to give thanks to God for his blessings and provision since 1677, when the first regular Thanksgiving proclamation was printed in Massachusetts.

It soon became an annual custom to set aside a day of Thanksgiving in all the colonies. President George Washington's first Thanksgiving proclamation in an official act reads, "Whereas it is the duty of all nations to acknowledge the Providence of Almighty God, to obey His will, to be grateful for His benefits, and humbly implore His protection and favor..." The proclamation goes on to call the nation to thankfulness to God. In 1864, President Abraham Lincoln issued a proclamation appointing the fourth Thursday of November, with a view of having the day kept annually thereafter without interruption.[12]

Many of our great leaders have expressed deep religious conviction. America's great lawmaker Daniel Webster said, "I believe Jesus Christ to be the Son of God; I believe that there is no other way of salvation than through the merits of His atonement. I believe that the Bible is to be understood and read."

Andrew Jackson also knew the importance of the Bible when he remarked to a friend, "That Book, sir, is the rock on which our republic rests."[13] We need more of this kind of commitment in our government leaders today.

America must not forget from whence she came. God's warning to the Israelites in Deuteronomy 8:10, 11, 18, 19 is equally applicable to America today: "When you have eaten and are satisfied, you shall bless the Lord your God for the good land which He has given you. Beware lest you forget the Lord your God by not keeping His commandments and His ordinances and statutes which I am commanding you today...

"But you shall remember the Lord your God, for it is He who is giving you power to make wealth, that He may confirm His covenant which He swore to your fathers, as it is this day. And it shall come about if you ever forget the Lord your God, and go after other gods and serve them and worship them, I testify against you today that you shall surely perish."

I do not want this nation to perish. But, like the nation of Israel, America has forgotten God and awaits His judgment. To avoid that judgment, we need to see renewal in all of our institutions, including the government.

We can see change in the government by following the method suggested earlier. If we can develop healthy models, evangelize people of influence and speak out against immorality, we can see fundamental moral change in our government. I believe the result will be great blessing to this nation.

We need to develop healthy models in government.

More and more we are seeing godly men run for office and become elected. But we need to see still more men and women in public office who will represent the interests of Christians and live a life-style that is honoring to the Lord.

The Moral Majority has done a lot of work in this area. At times members of the group have made over-generalizations and have made some seemingly gray issues appear white. But at least they have tried to speak out. They have been in the middle of some controversies and have become unpopular with many people. But then, throughout Bible times, urging people to return to morality often has not been popular. The push for Christians to become involved in politics and vote for candidates who fairly reflect the Judaeo-Christian morality is a commendable effort. As individual Christians,. we need to be involved in making our convictions known at the ballot box. And we shouldn't just wait for national elections, but vote our convictions on local issues as well.

Perhaps God would have you not only vote your convictions, but voice them as a candidate for an elected office. Maybe He would have you run for office in the PTA, the school board, or other positions in city and county government. We need to get involved in the government and model the kind of behavior we want to see in our leaders.

We need to evangelize people of influence in government.

Some exciting things have happened in this area, as many influential leaders at the national level have expressed an interest in learning more about Christ and growing in their relationship with Him. "The Fellowship" and Campus Crusade's Christian Embassy has seen some outstanding results in ministering to the spiritual needs of government officials in Washington.

These dedicated Christian workers minister to people of a wide variety of political persuasion. Their purposes are spiritual in nature, not political. And God has blessed their efforts.

One Campus Crusade staff member visited a senator in his office. "Within a few minutes it seemed as if we had known each other for a lifetime," the staff member remarked. "I asked him if he was a Christian and shared the gospel with him through the Four Spiritual Laws. Within 10 to 15 minutes after I had entered his office, he said he would like to receive Christ."

Not only are many of these people in government interested in receiving Christ, but they also are desirous of being trained to live a more effective Christian life. One leading senator was informed about a 14-hour Christian training session. The Campus Crusade staff member who invited the senator said he would understand if he were too busy to attend all of the sessions. The senator replied, "If I'm too busy to take this training, I'm too busy. There is nothing more important. When can I begin?"

Similar outreaches need to be started on the state level. Businessman and former state senator Arch Decker has begun such an evangelistic and discipleship ministry with legislators in Denver. Perhaps this is an area in which God would have you to be involved in your home state.

We need to speak out against immorality in government.

A group called "Salt and Pepper" is doing this in Portland, Oregon. Made up of influential Christian men in the city, the group comes together to speak out on political and social issues. Additional groups that speak out include the Pittsburgh Coalition in Ligonier, Pennsylvania; "Salt and Light" in Atlanta, Georgia; *Evangelical Newsletter* and *Washington & World Religion Report* are excellent in keeping you abreast of the issues that affect Christians (see appendix for addresses).

We need to see fundamental moral change in government.

For too long the words *corrupt* and *politician* have gone together like *peanut* and *butter*. In the wake of Watergate, Koreagate and Abscam, credibility of government leaders has plunged even further. Frank Mankiewicz, president of National Public Radio, describes this plunge: "In the 1960's, 70% of Americans had a favorable view of their government, generally trusted elected officials, and expected them to tell the truth. By the mid-1970's, the figure was only 30% according to social science surveys."[14]

This trend needs to change. And if we as Christians will pray, become involved and vote our convictions, the situation can be turned around.

Let me say again that I am highly encouraged by the trends in Washington, D.C. today. Thank God for similar trends at state and local levels. But the problems enumerated in this chapter are deep-rooted. We must not have any false euphoria. There is much to do. And you need to be involved like never before. It may mean life or death to us as a nation.

Action Points

1. Search the Word of God and other key books on issues relating to government.
2. Use your voting power to get the right people involved in government at various levels.
3. Get involved yourself in government through school boards, city council or county elected offices.

RECOMMENDED READING

Listen America! Jerry Falwell, Doubleday & Company

Death of a Nation, John Stormer, The Liberty Bell Press

Save America, Edward Rowe, Spire Books

Moral Majority, 499 South Capitol St., Ste. 101, Washington, D.C. 20003

Evangelical Newsletter, 1716 Spruce St., Philadelphia PA 19103

Washington World & Religion Report, Washington Building, Washington, D.C. 20005

CHAPTER TWELVE

Needed: Aware, Involved Christians

> ...all that is now necessary for the complete triumph of apostate secular humanism in the United States...is for Christians in America to sit back in their church pews, sing hymns and do absolutely nothing outside in the work-a-day world of business, education, labor and politics.—E.L. Hebden Taylor[1]

One of the major reasons our society has adopted a humanistic world view is that the Church has lost its dynamic impact on society. It is no longer serving as the salt of the earth and the light of the world. Let's take a closer look at the word pictures of salt and light that Christ used.

In Matthew 5, Christ gave some specific commands to His followers. He said, "You are the salt of the earth; but if the salt has become tasteless, how will it be made salty again? It is good for nothing any more, except to be thrown out and trampled under foot by men. You are the light of the world.

"A city set on a hill cannot be hidden. Nor do men light a lamp, and put it under the peck-measure, but on the lampstand; and it gives light to all who are in the house. Let your light shine before men in such a way that they may see your good works, and glorify your Father who is in heaven."

Light does three things. First of all it illuminates the darkness. Then it explains the darkness. And finally it shows how to get out of the darkness. In our day, many Christians no longer shine brightly; they are practically indistinguishable from the darkness that is this world.

Now let's look at salt. Like light, it too has several functions. First, it creates a thirst. Most of us have had the experience of eating some heavily salted food and soon thereafter becoming thirsty. Christians should have that same effect on the world. Their lives should be so exciting that non-Christians simply thirst to have what these Christians have.

Second, salt can be used as a preservative. In Jesus' day there were no refrigerators, so large quantities of salt were rubbed into meat. This prevented decay-causing bacteria from flourishing and enabled people to store meat for long periods of time without refrigeration. In the same way, a Christian is said to be a preservative. He is to be a deterrent to moral decay in our society.

Third, salt is used as seasoning; it adds flavor to food. Scientists tell us that salt is one of the most stable elements in nature and rarely loses its flavor. In Jesus' day, salt was carried in a pouch. It often became mixed with dust and sand and when it was time for the salt to be used on meat, the mixture had to be poured out. Too often, American Christians are like this residue instead of like useful salt which can be absorbed into our society and can flavor our culture.

The Christians of America have lost their savor. This is obvious from a recent Gallup Poll reporting that 53.4 percent of America's population claimed to have had a "born again" experience, and yet America's society in no way reflects the flavor of that much salt. If 53.4 percent of 100 bowls of soup were properly salted, you would surely notice the difference. And yet in today's society, the flavor of salt is barely noticeable.

This is in direct contrast to what happened to England as a result of those who came to know Christ through the ministry of John Wesley in the 1700's. John W. Prince writes of England during this time:

> England was at a low ebb morally and spiritually. Lawlessness, crime and immorality were increasing steadily. Heavy drinking was common in all classes of society and gambling particularly in the upper circles. Government was corrupt. The churches and the clergy were on the whole lifeless, and such religion as there was could not inspire any change in conditions, so superficial was it. The masses were in deep proverty and were shamefully neglected. Nothing needed a revival so much as religion.[2]

It was at this time that John Wesley came upon the

scene. God used him mightily to spark a great religious revival. For more thatn 50 years, Wesley traveled across Great Britain, preaching some 40,000 sermons and covering some 225,000 miles.

In addition, Wesley started Methodist societies wherever he went, meeting with them later to help supervise and encourage the minister and lay helpers. He also wrote several books on the issues of the day, such as slavery, smuggling and war. He also encouraged prison reform and was called "the first great friend to the poor."

God used John Wesley as His chosen instrument to help spark revival in the hearts of the people of England. And as the years went by, this revival of heart led people to see the need of putting political and social wrongs right again.

Historian J.R. Green writes of this period in *A Whole History of the English People*:

> In the nation at large appeared a new moral enthusiasm which, rigid and pedantic as it often seemed, was still healthy in its social tone, and whose power was seen in the disappearance of the profligacy which had disgraced the upper classes, and the foulness which had invested literature, ever since the Restoration. A yet nobler result of the religious revival was the steady attempt...to remedy the guilt, the ignorance, the physical suffering, the social degradation of the profligate and the poor. It was not till the Wesleyan impulse had done its work that this philanthropic impulse began.

One social reform after another swept the land after the Wesleyan revival. The abolition of slavery was just one of them. Wesley called slavery "a scandal, not only to Christianity but to humanity." In 1750 most people thought it was a benefit to society, but by 1833 it had been outlawed.

During the Wesleyan revival and in the years that followed, the Christians in England acted as the salt of the earth and the light of the world. Without question they made an impact on their society. Even historians recognized it.

Why isn't this same sort of impact being made on our society by most American Christians? Two reasons come to mind. First, we are unaware of God's purpose for us here on earth. Second, we are uninvolved in living the kind of life that God wants us to live.

Christians, as the Body of Christ, are unaware of who we are in Christ and what God's purpose is for us. We are God's children. We are set aside for His purposes. Our citizenship is in heaven. We are called to be rulers in that we are to "subdue the earth," as the Bible says in the first chapter of Genesis.

Do you get the feeling we are special? We are indeed special in God's sight, and we should be in our sight too. As special people we should have an upbeat, positive outlook on life. Too often, Christians have a downcast, defeatist attitude and they communicate this to the world.

A fellow I talked with once on a plane had gotten that message from somewhere. "Oh, you're a Christian," he said, with a tone of voice that suggested I must have foam rubber for brains. I turned and looked at him feigning the same kind of disgust he had projected.

"You're *not?*" I asked. "Why do you look at me with disgust and ask me if I'm a Christian? I've got everything to win and nothing to lose, if I'm a Christian. I've got an authority. I believe in the Word of God. Scripture says I'm an ambassador.

"I'm holy and righteous in God's eyes. I'm seated at the right hand of the Father. I'm a special person. I've got a full inheritance while I'm on this earth, and when I die I'll live with God forever and I'll rule with God for eternity. That's what I've got. What have you got?"

My purpose, of course, was not to demean another person, but to show that the Christian has *everything* going for him while the non-Christian has *nothing* going for him.

We are important! I tried to communicate that fact in an innovative way to another man I sat beside on a plane. When he asked me what I did, I told him, "I'm an ambassador."

"You're a what?" he asked.

"I'm an ambassador."

"What country do you represent?" he asked.

"Oh, I represent something far larger than a country."

"Do you represent a region, or a continent?"

I replied, "Far greater than a region or a continent."

"What do you represent?"

"I represent a kingdom."

"What kind of kingdom?"

"I represent the kingdom of God. I'm an ambassador of Christ." From that point I went on to tell him about Christ.

We should act as ambassadors of Christ. If we were the son or daughter of the President of the United States, that would greatly affect how we talked and acted—knowing that what we said and did would reflect on him. In the same way, we are God's representatives here on earth. Wherever I am, I am to represent the God of the universe.

Our purpose in being here on earth is to glorify God. How do we do that? The most strategic way to glorify God while on earth is to live in light of eternity. The Bible says to "set your mind on the things above, not on the things that are on earth."[3] "Lay up for yourselves treasures in heaven..."[4]

As Christians, we are called to become holy, righteous men and women. "Seek ye first the kingdom of God and His *righteousness*; and all these things shall be added unto you."[5] We need to seek to be righteous. The Word of God will last forever, and the extent to which we get the Word built into our lives through the power of the Spirit determines our capacity to glorify God throughout eternity.

Influencing People

The second thing we are to do is to influence the maximum number of people in the maximum way. We are to have the utmost impact on people because we are to seek first the kingdom of God or the rule of Christ in the lives of people.

Only two things on this earth will last forever—the Word of God and people. So, we need to spend our time concentrating on these two things. Scripture says that our time here on earth, compared to eternity, is like a vapor. The critical question is, "How am I spending my time?" When I die, I don't have the option to sit down and try to do it again. We'll have to answer the question, "Did you spend your life wisely for eternity?"

In addition to our being unaware of who we are in Christ and His purpose for us here on earth, we are unaware of what's happening in our culture. We are struggling in a battle with Satan, and many of us are not aware of it.

In his book *Save America!*, Edward Rowe asks the question:

Why have Christians so often been so blind to the meaning of the great events transpiring in our time? Is it because we haven't bothered to relate the Word of God to those affairs of life which lie beyond our personal interests, our families and our immediate circle of Christian friends?

Rowe cites a tragic historical example of this taking place in Nazi Germany. A Christian who had lived through the war told Rowe, "Most of the Bible-believing Christians of Germany were right on Hitler's bandwagon at the time of his rise to power. They felt that he made more sense than anyone else, that he was unifying the country, that he had a clear-cut plan in a time of deep confusion.

"These Christians were so busy with their Bible studies, their prayer meetings, their worship services, and their Christian fellowship that they were almost totally unaware of the controlling realities of the time."

Some of these same failings are present in Christians today. We are unaware of what is going on in our society, and we have ceased to think biblically. Satan has deluded the minds of many Christians. A definite battle for the mind is going on, and society is one of the weapons Satan uses in his warfare.

Uninvolved

In addition to being unaware, many Christians are uninvolved in living the kind of life God wants us to live. As I mentioned earlier, many Americans have adopted an attitude of phony pietism. They have separated themselves from the things that concern our Lord. This can have disastrous consequences.

We Christians need to be involved in the burning moral issues of our day. We need to hold up the Bible and say there is an absolute standard of right and wrong. We are against homosexuality, for example, not just because of the sociological implications, but because the Word of God says it's wrong.

People need to see that there are some absolutes. Relativism is so pervasive in our society that people have forgotten there are absolutes. The Bible not only shows there are certain things that are wrong, but it gives solutions as well.

People are looking for an authority, and we need to hold up the Word of God as that authority. That means I hold it up against homosexuality, abortion, divorce and other issues that the Bible speaks out against. Some people ask, "How can you hold up a Christian standard in a non-Christian world? This is a pluralistic society."

My answer would be that our standard is absolute truth and as such relates to the Christian and the non-Christian regardless of how pluralistic our society is. Even if our society is pagan the biblical standard is still valid.

An example of this is found in the life and ministry of the Old Testament prophet Amos. He held up the biblical standard not only for Judah and Israel but also for six neighboring Gentile nations. As James McHann points out in his article, "A Time for Sackcloth and Ashes?". "An important point emerges from Amos' message: God is the sovereign Lord of all the nations and holds them accountable for living according to His moral law. When they do not, He pours out His wrath upon them."[6]

Like Amos, the Christian community needs to hold up the biblical standard. And the most visible display of that standard is for Christians to let their convictions be demonstrated in every aspect of their lives.

Commitment to Christ demands holistic, righteous living. By righteous living, I mean getting the Word of God into my life in the power of the Holy Spirit; being involved in evangelism (taking the good news about Christ to others) and discipleship (helping others to grow in their faith).

Currently there is a lack of discipleship in many lives. A number of people are coming to Christ but are not genuinely making Him Lord of their lives.

Finally, there is a lack of dealing with the social issues, those issues which are of concern to our Lord. As Christians recognize who they are in Christ and take definite actions to be involved in our culture, we can see change take place in society.

We have talked about the need for good models, the need to evangelize strategic people, the need to speak out and the need to see fundamental change. This must take place in each of America's institutions.

Several foundational strategies are essential in effecting this transformation of the family, education, government, the media and religion. The first of these strategies involves the creation of an international think tank. This group would look over all of America's institutions and continue to do research on these facets of American life. They would also "brainstorm" on ideas for influencing key areas.

In a recent brainstorming session, a number of us began pooling ideas on how Christians could influence the media. We came up with some innovative methods that could prove very effective:

— form Christian-owned TV networks/newspapers;
— support good ones currently in operation;
— lobby against advertisers of objectionable programming;
— identify power structures in the media and get Christians to become a part of those structures;
— re-educate the public on what to expect from the media;
— investigate future trends in TV;
— develop a strategy of community action in dealing with renewal of local stations' licenses;
— develop artistically produced feature films.

Another purpose of this think tank would be to discover who are the leaders in the various institutions of America and to consider ways of influencing them for Christ. In addition, the think tank would research institutions from a biblical perspective and publish books and newsletters revealing their findings. Then finally, this group would coordinate and stimulate positive action to bring about change.

The second of the foundational strategies would be to determine existing leadership and get them trained and mobilized for action. In addition, we need to train a new breed of leader for each sphere of leadership through graduate education — a leader who can think biblically, minister strategically, live morally and penetrate his sphere of influence with the reality of Christ's teaching and presence. This dream has prompted Dr. Bill Bright to begin the International Christian Graduate University. It is geared to meet this specific and strategic need.

Once these leaders and their spheres of influence are pinpointed, we need to be sending them newsletters. This medium would begin ministering to these people, give them a sense of being a part of a group and also would inform them of how they could help solve some of our society's problems.

After the leaders have been targeted and informed through newsletters, conferences need to be developed for each area. Gatherings need to be held, bringing together leaders in government, law and other fields. These conferences would be solution-oriented and give the delegates a biblical perspective on their position. The conferences also would offer ideas for positive steps leaders could take to begin influencing their areas for Christ.

Another foundation strategy is consulting. This approach would be similar to the use of consultants in the business world where experts come into a business and advise the management in the consultant's area of expertise. In the same way, those who are "experts" in having an impact for Christ in their sphere of influence would be available as consultants to advise other leaders in how they could use their position to have a maximum influence for Christ.

The fifth foundational strategy would be to use the method of networking to reach the key leaders in our society. That is, those involved in reaching similar target groups need to get together to exchange ideas, to encourage one another and to determine ways they can saturate their spheres of influence with the message of Christ.

As Christians, we need to promote an atmosphere where this kind of networking will take place. For instance, one man I know is the manager of the leading Christian radio station in Philadelphia. He is having quite an impact for Christ in that area. And now he's starting to work with others in similar positions in other parts of the country to permeate their areas with the Christian message. Newsletters can assist in networking by communicating what different individuals are doing. This will enable the key people to find out what is being successful and implement it in their own locale.

Several strategies have been presented to help firmly plant the case of Christ in the institutions of America. We want to see Christian lifestyles, biblically-based decisions and Christ-honoring results spring up from the seeds we plant. But we will see no yield unless we plant a seed. Start out by choosing one of the areas we've discussed, and choose one strategy to plant in that area.

Perhaps God would have you aid in the development of healthy models. Maybe He would have you reach some strategic people. God might want you to speak out about immorality. Or he might desire you to be used to help bring about fundamental change.

Drawing on the inexhaustible resources and wisdom of God's Holy Spirit, make your choice. Then plant that embryonic strategy in the field of the family, education, government, media, business or religion. Throw yourself enthusiastically behind your choice. Recruit others to join with you. God might choose to bless your efforts with abundant results: 30-, 60- or a hundredfold.

The family, education, government, the media and the church can be transformed. What happened in John Wesley's England—reawakening, renewal and restoration—can happen in America today. I look forward to that day—a day when Christians are vigorously seasoning our society with the flavor of Christ; a day when the Body of Christ is a floodlight on a busy thoroughfare, illuminating the path to the Savior for many; a day when believers are engulfed by the love and power of their living Lord.

Action Points

1. List the following items on a sheet of paper and rate them (by circling appropriate number) as to how true they are of your life:
   a) Unaware of who you are in Christ   1 2 3 4 5
   b) Unaware of what is happening in
      our culture   1 2 3 4 5
   c) Uninvolved in moral issues   1 2 3 4 5
2. Focus on one of these areas to trust God to bring your life more in keeping with His standards.

RECOMMENDED READING

Measure of a Church, Gene Getz, Regal Books

The Dynamics of Church Growth, Ron Jenson and Jim Stevens, Baker

The Community of the King, Howard A. Snyder, IV Press

Father Power, Henry Biller and Dennis Meredith, Anchor Books

Dad's Only newsletter 3407 Highway 79, Julian, CA 92036

Tough and Tender, Joyce Landorf

Measure of a Woman, Gene Getz, Regal Books

"Assignment Life," New Liberty Films, 1805 W. Magnolia Blvd., Burbank, CA (This film portrays abortion as it really takes place and is a powerful statement on why abortion should be stopped)

Our Dance Has Turned to Death, Carl Wilson, Renewal Publishing Company

Concerned Women for America, P. O. Box 20376, El Cajon, CA 92021 (newsletter)

NOTES

CHAPTER 1

1. Tim Timmons, *Maximum Living in a Pressure-Cooker World*, Word, Waco, Texas, 1979, p. 13;
2. Gerald Kennedy, *A Reader's Notebook*, New York, New York, 1953, p. 224;
3. Jerry Falwell, *Listen America!* Doubleday & Co., Garden City, New York, 1980, p. 25;
4. Dr. James Dobson, "Focus on the Family" Film series, film 3
5. Dr. Charles Malik, "America at the Crossroads of History," *Worldwide Challenge*, January, 1980, p. 7;
6. "Public Schools, They're Destroying Our Children", *American Opinion*, Belmont, Massachusetts, February, 1972, p. 1;
7. Timmons, *op. cit.*, p. 111, 112.

CHAPTER 2

1. Woody Allen, "Adrift Alone in the Cosmos," December, 1979. *Reader's Digest*, p. 167;
2. Francis Schaeffer and C. Everett Koop, *Whatever Happened to the Human Race?*, Fleming H. Revell, Old Tappan, New Jersey, 1979, p. 21;
3. Homer Duncan, *Secular Humanism; the Most Dangerous Religion in America*, Missionary Crusader, Lubbock, Texas, 1979, p. 13;
4. *Humanist Manifesto II*, Prometheus Books, Buffalo, New York, 1973;
5. *Ibid.*
6. Schaeffer and Koop, *op. cit.*;
7. Duncan, *op. cit.*, p. 46;
8. Tim LaHaye, *The Battle for the Mind*, Old Tappan, New Jersey, Fleming H. Revell, 1980, p. 179.

CHAPTER 3

1. "Schaeffer's Advice for Layleaders," *Eternity* September, 1980, p. 23;
2. P.J. Johnstone, *Operation World*, STL Publications, Kent, England, 1978, p. 26;
3. Ron Jenson, *How to Succeed the Biblical Way*, Wheaton, Illinois, Tyndale House, 1981, p. 33-34;
4. *Ibid.*, p. 77.

CHAPTER 4

1. "Sinfully Together," *Time*, July 9, 1979, p. 55;
2. "Violent Families," *Time*, July 9, 1979, p. 55;
3. *Ibid.*
4. *The Pantagraphy*, September 20, 1970;
5. "How Gay is Gay?" *Time*, April 23, 1979, p. 72,73;
6. Jim Morud, "Hope for the Homosexual," *Worldwide Challenge*, September, 1980, p. 38,39;

7. "The Children of Divorce," Newsweek, February 11, 1980, p. 61;
8. *Ibid.*
9. "The American Family: Bent – But Not Broken," *U.S. News & World Report,* June 16, 1980.
10. "The Children of Divorce," *op. cit.*, p. 59;
11. *Ibid.*, p. 61;
12. Dr. James Dobson, "Focus on the Family" film series, Film 3;
13. James Robison, *Attack on the Family*, Wheaton, Illinois, Tyndale House, 1980, p. 27;
14. Francis A. Schaeffer and C. Everett Koop, M.D. *Whatever Happened to the Human Race?*, Old Tappan, New Jersey, Fleming Revell Co., 1978, p. 30;
15. "The Problem of the Abused and Neglected Child," Information Services, California Departmen of Justice, August, 1976, p. 6;
16. Schaeffer and Koop, *op. cit.*, p. 30;
17. Steven S. Foster, "You Can Help Prevent Child Abuse," *Worldwide Challenge*, October, 1980, p. 32, 33;
18. "Child Pornography; Outrage Starts to Stir Some Action," *U.S. News & World Report*, June 12, 1977, p. 66;
19. Melinda Blau, "Why Parents Kick Their Kids Out," *Parents' Magazine,*
20. James Berry, "Why They Run," *Parents' Magazine*, April, 1979, p. 68.

CHAPTER 5

1. "Bob and Trudy Kruse," *Worldwide Challenge*, April, 1979, p. 16, 17;
2. *Reader's Digest*, February, 1981, p. 104;
3. Steven S. Foster, "Being an Effective Father," *Worldwide Challenge*, June, 1981, p. 9, 10;
4. Mark 14:36;
5. James E. Kilgore, "Making Your Marriage Divorce-Proof," *Family Life Today*;
6. Basil Miller, *John Wesley*, Minneapolis, Bethany Fellowship Inc., 1943, p. 12, 15.

CHAPTER 6

1. Jim Buchfuehrer, "Action Alternatives," *Plan for Action: An Action Alternative Handbook for Whatever Happened to the Human Race?* Old Tappan New Jersey, Fleming H. Revell, 1978, p. 28;
2. Francis A. Schaeffer and C. Everett Koop, M.D. *Whatever Happened to the Human Race?*, Old Tappan, New Jersey, Fleming H. Revell Company, 1978, p. 34;
3. "The Fanatical Abortion Fight," *Time*, July 9, 1979, p. 26;
4. EP News, January 19, 1980, p. 4;
5. *Op. cit.*, *Time*, p. 27;
6. Schaeffer and Koop, *op. cit.*, p. 41,42;
7. EP News Service, June 14, 1980, p. 11;
8. *Fort Lauderdale News*, November 13, 1977;
9. Schaeffer and Koop, *op. cit.*, p. 61;
10. *Ibid.*, p. 64;

11. C. Everett Koop, M.D., "The Gravity of the Situation," *Plan for Action: An Action Alternative for Whatever Happened to the Human Race?*, Old Tappan New Jersey, Fleming H. Revell, 1978, p. 46;

12. *Ibid.*

13. *Medical Tribune*, October 10, 1973;

14. Schaeffer and Koop, *op. cit.*, p. 106;

15. Francis Schaeffer, *Back to Freedom and Dignity*, Downer Grove, Ill., Inter-Varsity Press, 1972, p. 1;

16. Tim Timmons, *Maximum Living in a Pressure-Cooker World*, Waco, Texas, Word Books, 1979, p. 60;

17. *Ibid.*, p. 64;

18. Francis Schaeffer, "The Common Questions," *Plan for Action: An Action Alternative Handbook for Whatever Happened to the Human Race?*, Old Tappan, New Jersey, Fleming H. Revell, 1978, p. 76;

19. Walter Isaacson, "The Battle Over Abortion," *Time*, April 6, 1981, p. 24.

CHAPTER 7

1. Peter Marshall and David Manuel, *The Light and the Glory*, Old Tappan, New Jersey, Fleming H. Revell Company, 1977, p. 252;

2. *Ibid.*, p. 248;

3. EP News Service, June 7, 1980, p. 1;

4. Kenneth S. Kantzer, "The Charismatics Among Us," *Christianity Today*, February 22, 1980, p. 25;

5. "Cults: Are Teens Being Brainwashed?" *Seventeen*, May, 1979, p. 78;

6. *People*, December 4, 1978, p. 87-94;

7. "Following the Leader," *Time*, December 11, 1978, p. 36;

8. Margaret Singer, "Coming Out of the Cults," *Psychology Today*, January 1979, p. 72;

9. *People*, op. cit., p. 87-94;

10. EP News Service, May 31, 1980, p. 11;

11. Tim Timmons, *Maximum Living in a Pressure-Cooker World*, Waco, Texas, Word Books, 1979, p. 97, 98;

12. Hal Lindsey, *Satan is Alive and Well on Planet Earth*, Grand Rapids, Michigan, Zondervan, 1972, p. 18-20.

13. John A. Stormer, *Death of a Nation*, Florissant, Missouri, The Liberty Bell Press, 1968, p. 96, 97;

14. "A U.N. on Its Knees," *Time*, November 24, 1975, p. 77;

15. EP News Service, June 7, 1980, p. 4;

16. Kathy Rebello-Rees, *San Bernardino Sun*, "Gay Minister Stresses Changing the Churches," July 23, 1979;

17. EP News Service, January 5, 1980, p. 1;

18. Dale Dawson, "I've Made America What She Is Today," *Worldwide Challenge*, July, 1976, p. 18.

CHAPTER 8

1. A.W. Tozer, *The Pursuit of God*, Harrisburg, Pennsylvania, Christian Publications, p. 69;

2. *Ibid.*, p. 67;
3. "Who Are the Nation's Leaders Today?" *Time*, August 6, 1979, p. 29;
4. Bishop Ryle, *Practical Religion*, London, James Clark & Co., 1959, p. 130.

CHAPTER 9

1. "The ABCs of School Violence," *Time*, January 23, 1978, p. 73;
2. "Now It's Suburbs Where School Violence Flares," *U.S. News & World Report*, May 21, 1979, p. 63;
3. Tim LaHaye, *The Battle for the Mind*, Old Tappan, New Jersey, Fleming Revell, 1980, p. 44;
4. "Teacher Can't Teach," *Time*, June 16, 1980, p. 55;
5. *Ibid.*, p. 58;
6. *Ibid.*, p. 59
7. *Ibid.*, p. 56;
8. "Chasing Ghosts," *Time*, August 27, 1979;
9. "Teacher Can't Teach," *op. cit.*, p. 59;
10. "The Case of the Missing Millions," *Time*, December 17, 1979, p. 77;
11. Sidney B. Simon, Leland W. Howe, Howard Kirschenbaum, *Values Clarification: A Handbook of Practical Strategies for Teachers and Students*, New York, New York, Hart Publishing Company, 1972, p. 20;
12. *Newsweek*, June 2, 1980, p. 58;
13. "Are Public Schools About to Flunk?" *U.S. News & World Report*, June 8, 1981, p. 59;
14. "A Beacon of Integrated Excellence," *Sports Illustrated*, February 23, 1981, p. 72;
15. Robert L. Cleath, "Needed: Christian Professors Who Profess," *Christianity Today*, May 23, 1974, p. 11;1
16. Charles Malik, "The Other Side of Evangelism," *Christianity Today*, November 7, 1980, p. 40.

CHAPTER 10

1. *Time*, May 28, 1979, p. 50;
2. Dave Boehi, "The Show Goes On (And On and On)," *Worldwide Challenge*, November, 1978, p. 7;
3. Dan Maust "You Don't Have to Ride the Tide," *Worldwide Challenge*, March 1981, p. 50;
4. *Ibid.*
5. *Ibid.*

CHAPTER 11

1. Tim Timmons, *Maximum Living in a Pressure-Cooker World*, Word Books, Waco, Texas, 1979, p. 177;
2. "Is America Strong Enough?" *Newsweek*, October 27, 1980, p. 48;
3. *Ibid.*
4. "The Salt Syndrome," produced by the American Security Council;

5. Jerry Falwell, *Listen, America!*, Doubleday & Co., Garden City, N.Y. 1980, p. 12;

6. *Ibid.*, p. 51;

7. "Red Tape: It's Bad at Grass Roots, Too," September 24, 19, p. 69;

8. Timmons, *op cit.*, p. 11-112;

9. Falwell, *op. cit.*, p. 12;

10. Falwell, *op. cit.*, p. 38;

11. "Morality...Courage...Common Sense—Qualities Leaders Need Most," *U.S. News & World Report*, April 19, 1976, p. 29;

12. Falwell, *op. cit.*, p. 46;

13. *Ibid.*, p. 47;

14. "Americans Distrust Their Leaders," *USA Today*, April, 1979, p. 2.

CHAPTER 12

1. E.L. Hebdon Taylor, *Religious Neutrality in Politics.*

2. John W. Prince, "John Wesley," *Founders of Christian Movements*, Edited by Phillip Lotz. Books for Libraries Press, Freeport, New York, 1941, p. 153;

3. Colossians 3:2

4. Matthew 6:19

5. Matthew 6:33 (King James)

6. James McHann, "A Time for Sackcloth and Ashes?" *Worldwide Challenge*, March 1980, p. 8.

---

end notes